9/14
35.00

How to Use This Book

Look for these special features in this book:

SIDEBARS, **CHARTS**, **GRAPHS**, and original **MAPS** expand your understanding of what's being discussed—and also make useful sources for classroom reports.

FAQs answer common **F**requently **A**sked **Q**uestions about people, places, and things.

WOW FACTORS offer "Who knew?" facts to keep you thinking.

TRAVEL GUIDE gives you tips on exploring the state—either in person or right from your chair!

PROJECT ROOM provides fun ideas for school assignments and incredible research projects. Plus, there's a guide to primary sources—what they are and how to cite them.

Please note: All statistics are as up-to-date as possible at the time of publication.
Population data is taken from the 2010 census.

Consultants: Marvin Bergman, State Historical Society of Iowa; William Loren Katz;
Brian Witzke, Iowa Geological Survey; Millie K. Frese, Education and Outreach Manager,
State Historical Museum of Iowa

Book production by The Design Lab

Library of Congress Cataloging-in-Publication Data
Blashfield, Jean F.
  Iowa / by Jean F. Blashfield. — Revised edition.
  pages cm. — (America the beautiful, third series)
  Includes bibliographical references and index.
  Audience: Ages 9–12.
  ISBN 978-0-531-28279-3 (lib. bdg.)
  1. Iowa—Juvenile literature. I. Title.
  F621.3.B58 2014
  977.7—dc23   2013044318

1 2 3 4 5 6 7 8 9 10 R 24 23 22 21 20 19 18 17 16 15

AMERICA ★ THE ★ BEAUTIFUL

Iowa

BY JEAN F. BLASHFIELD

Third Series, Revised Edition

Children's Press®
An Imprint of Scholastic Inc.
New York ★ Toronto ★ London ★ Auckland ★ Sydney
Mexico City ★ New Delhi ★ Hong Kong
Danbury, Connecticut

CONTENTS

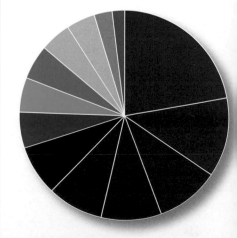

4 GROWTH AND CHANGE

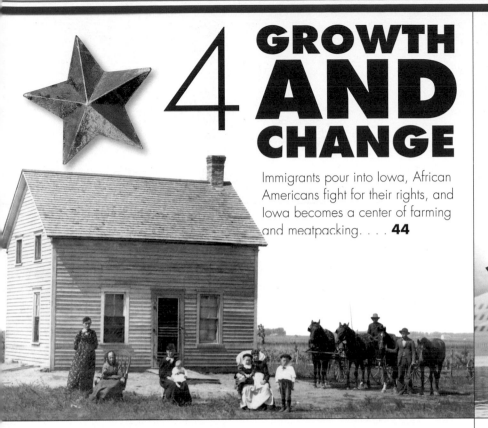

Immigrants pour into Iowa, African Americans fight for their rights, and Iowa becomes a center of farming and meatpacking. . . . **44**

5 MORE MODERN TIMES

Iowans survive wars and weather, people leave the countryside, and newcomers bring greater diversity to the state. **60**

9 TRAVEL GUIDE

Explore historic farms, inspect antique aircraft, and marvel at the beauty of bright hot air balloons against the crisp blue sky. There's plenty to keep you busy in Iowa. **106**

PROJECT ROOM

★

N
W E
S

MINNESOTA

WISCONSIN

Laura Ingalls
Wilder Museum

Big Sioux

Vesterheim
Norwegian-American Museum

DECORAH

Driftless

Wells' Dairy

MASON CITY

Area

Mississippi

SIOUX CITY

Cedar

Iowa

DUBUQUE

Missouri

National Farm
Toy Museum

Wapsipinicon

Little Sioux

WATERLOO

IOWA

Iowa State
Capitol

CEDAR RAPIDS

Herbert Hoover
National Historic Site

DeSoto National
Wildlife Refuge

Living History
Farms

DES MOINES

Devonian
Fossil Gorge

DAVENPORT

COUNCIL BLUFFS

Pella Historical
Village

Buffalo Bill
Museum

Iowa
State Fair

National Balloon
Museum

Mississippi Valley

NEBRASKA

Covered Bridges of
Madison County

Des Moines

Airpower Museum

Mississippi

Snake
Alley

ILLINOIS

MISSOURI

QUICK FACTS

State capital: Des Moines
Largest city: Des Moines
Total area: 56,273 square miles
(145,746 sq km)
Highest point: Hawkeye Point at
1,670 feet (509 m), in Osceola
County
Lowest point: 480 feet (146 m)
along the Mississippi River, in
Lee County

0   40
Miles

Welcome to Iowa!

HOW DID IOWA GET ITS NAME?

The state of Iowa was named for the Iowa River, and the river was named for the native Ioway people. The word *Ioway* has been interpreted many different ways. It has been translated as "yawners," "sleepy ones," "people across the river," "ashy heads," and even "dead-fish eaters." According to a historical report commissioned in 1870 by the Iowa legislature, the name means "the beautiful land." The report stated, "A band of Indians journeying towards the setting sun, reached the bank of the Great River that washes our eastern border, and looking across the broad water, beheld for the first time the green slopes of our beautiful prairies stretching away in the distance. Their exclamation was 'IOWA—the Beautiful Land!'"

IOWA

OHIO

INDIANA

KENTUCKY

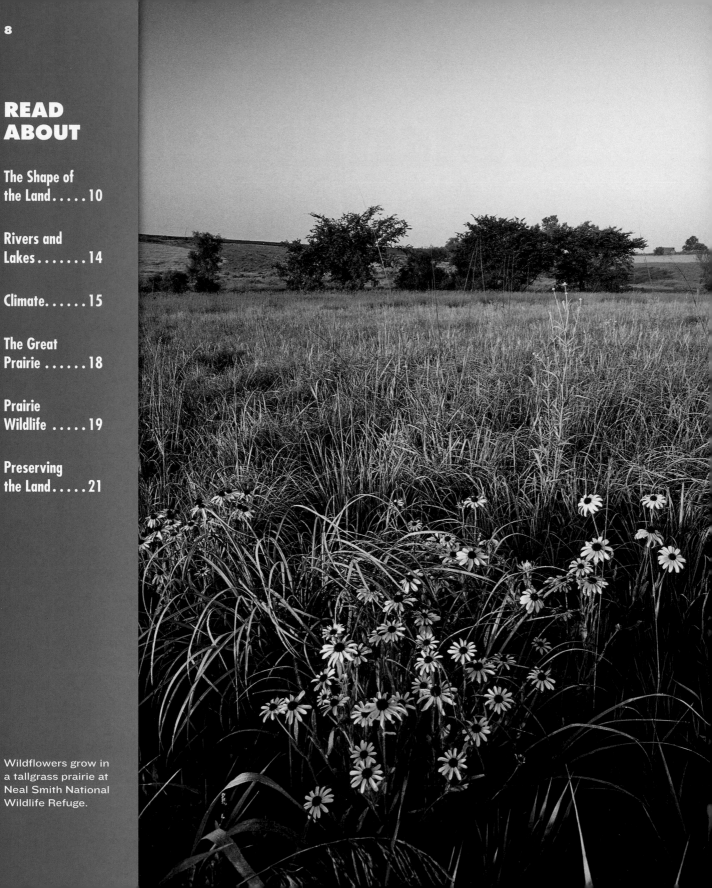

READ ABOUT

Wildflowers grow in a tallgrass prairie at Neal Smith National Wildlife Refuge.

LAND

★

TWO GREAT RIVERS FLANK THE STATE OF IOWA. The Mississippi River is to the east, and the Missouri River is to the west. They provide water for the state's 56,273 square miles (145,746 square kilometers) of land. Endless farm fields make Iowa seem flat, but mostly the land is gently rolling. Iowa's lowest point is 480 feet (146 meters) above sea level in the southeastern corner of the state, along the Mississippi River. Its highest point is Hawkeye Point at 1,670 feet (509 m) above sea level, in Osceola County in the northwest.

Limestone bluffs along the Upper Iowa River

WORD TO KNOW

alluvial plains *areas that are created when sand, soil, and rocks are carried by water and dropped in certain places*

THE SHAPE OF THE LAND

Iowa is famous for miles and miles of rolling farmland, but underneath the fields are seven different land regions. Each region has its own kind of soil.

Alluvial Plains

The **Alluvial Plains** lie along the Mississippi and Missouri rivers. This land is made up of soil, sand, and gravel that was left behind by the rivers when they flooded. The Alluvial Plains along the Missouri River are rolling hills, and some spectacular sandstone and limestone bluffs, or cliffs, rise along the Mississippi.

Iowa Topography

Use the color-coded elevation chart to see on the map Iowa's high points (orange) and low points (green). Elevation is measured as the distance above or below sea level.

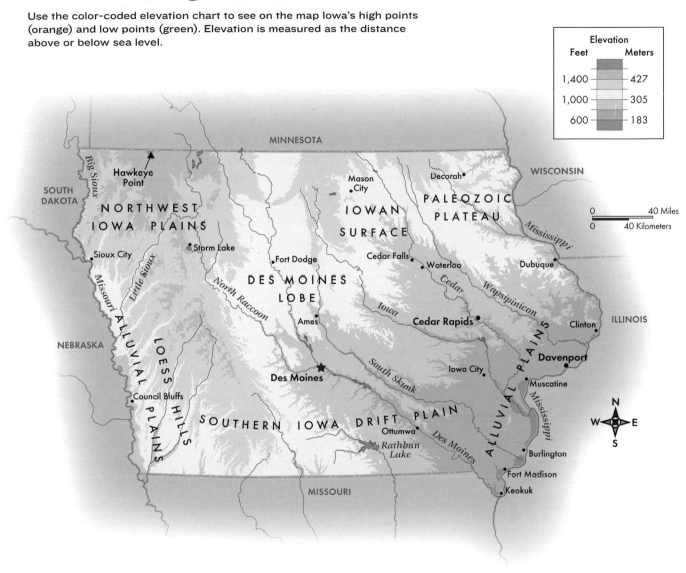

Elevation

Feet		Meters
1,400		427
1,000		305
600		183

Paleozoic Plateau

In the northeastern corner of the state is a raised area called the Paleozoic **Plateau**. The underlying rock dates to the Paleozoic Era, between 430 million and 500 million years ago. The rock has been deeply eroded, or worn away, into hills and steep valleys. This region includes

WORD TO KNOW

plateau *an elevated part of the earth with steep slopes*

Iowa Geo-Facts

Along with the state's geographical highlights, this chart ranks Iowa's land, water, and total area compared to all other states.

Total area; rank . . . . . 56,273 square miles (145,746 sq km); 26th
Land; rank . . . . .55,858 square miles (144,672 sq km); 23rd
Water; rank . . . . 415 square miles (1,075 sq km); 45th
Inland water; rank . . . . 415 square miles (1,075 sq km); 40th
Geographic center . . . Story County, 5 miles (8 km) northeast of Ames
Latitude . . . . 40°36' N to 43°30' N
Longitude . . . . 89°5' W to 96°31' W
Highest point . . . . Hawkeye Point at 1,670 feet (509 m), in Osceola County
Lowest point . . . . .480 feet (146 m) along the Mississippi River, in Lee County
Largest city . . . . Des Moines
Longest river . . . . Des Moines River, 525 miles (845 km)

Source: U.S. Census Bureau, 2010 census

 Rhode Island would fit inside Iowa more than 36 times! And Iowa would fit inside Alaska more than 11 times.

WORDS TO KNOW

sinkholes *natural depressions in the ground that form when underlying rocks are dissolved by groundwater*

moraines *deposits of earth and stones carried by a glacier and dropped*

drift *material left behind by a retreating glacier*

steep cliffs overlooking the Mississippi River. There are many caves and **sinkholes** in the rock.

Des Moines Lobe

About 14,000 years ago, a glacier reached down into what is now central Iowa. As the ice melted, it left behind **moraines** as well as depressions that today form the landscape. The land is also called Young **Drift** Plains.

The depressions gouged out by the retreating glacier became lake beds. Pioneers found the land so riddled with shallow lakes and wetlands that it was difficult to cross except in winter when the water was frozen. Farmers wanted to use the land, so they drained it. They put pipes and tiles below-ground. Water from surrounding soil would drain across the tiles and pipes, leaving usable soil behind. Much of Iowa's productive farmland was created this way.

Turning all this wetland into dry land destroyed habitat for many plants and animals. It also left many towns without a nearby lake, even though their names have the word *lake* in them. For example, the town of Lake City has no lake.

Iowan Surface

East of the Des Moines Lobe and wrapping around the Paleozoic Plateau is a region called the Iowan Surface.

Many Iowa plains have been transformed into productive farmland.

The land has a rolling surface with long slopes. In the north are depressions and sinkholes where soft limestone rock collapsed. Glaciers once covered this land, but they had formed well before the ice sheet that made the Des Moines Lobe.

Northwest Iowa Plains

West of the Des Moines Lobe and covering the northwestern corner of the state is the Northwest Iowa Plains. This area is higher and drier than the rest of the state and has fewer trees. The state's highest elevations are in this region.

THE DISAPPEARING HIGHEST SPOT

Ocheyedan Mound is a cone-shaped mound of sand and gravel that fell through a hole in a retreating glacier millions of years ago. It used to be Iowa's highest point. But in the 20th century, people removed so much sand and gravel from the mound that it shrank to second highest point. The new top spot, Hawkeye Point, is on a nearby farm in northwestern Iowa. It reaches 1,670 feet (509 m) above sea level.

WORDS TO KNOW

silt *fine particles of soil that are carried by flowing water and settle to the bottom of a river or lake*

reservoir *artificial lake or tank for storing water*

SEE IT HERE!

NATIONAL MISSISSIPPI RIVER MUSEUM AND AQUARIUM

Get a good look at the fish of the Upper Mississippi at the National Mississippi River Museum and Aquarium, located on the Mississippi in Dubuque. It includes six large aquariums that hold a variety of water creatures. Visitors can also get a firsthand look at the mighty river by taking a Wildlife Eco Cruise. You can explore a steamboat or spend the night on the *William M. Black*, a huge boat that dredged the Missouri River so that wartime craft could be transported on it. The museum also includes the National Rivers Hall of Fame, which highlights the pioneers, artists, and explorers closely associated with the nation's rivers.

Loess Hills

The Loess Hills run along the Missouri River inland from the Alluvial Plains. *Loess*, a German word for "loose," is a yellow-gray material made mostly of **silt**. The silt was deposited by rivers during periods of glacial melting and then blown by the wind. In Iowa, the wind drove the loess into deep piles—the Loess Hills, which rise abruptly from the Missouri River valley. In some areas, the soil made from the loess is 200 feet (61 m) deep. In general, trees grow on the northern and eastern slopes of these rough and beautiful hills, which are wetter than the other slopes. Prairie grasses and other plants grow on the south and west slopes.

Southern Iowa Drift Plain

The Southern Iowa Drift Plain covers the southern half of the state. Glaciers scoured the region long ago. The glacial deposits were then covered by loess. In the millions of years since glaciers covered the area, river valleys have cut into the land. Trees and small forests are found in the valleys.

RIVERS AND LAKES

The Mississippi and Missouri rivers define Iowa's eastern and western borders. Major rivers that flow through the state include the Des Moines, Iowa, and Cedar. The Des Moines River, which begins just across the border in Minnesota, flows through the state for 525 miles (845 km), making it the state's longest river.

Iowa's natural lakes are all in the Des Moines Lobe region. The three largest are Spirit Lake, West Okoboji Lake, and East Okoboji Lake. The state's other main lakes were formed when dams were built across rivers. The largest is Lake Red Rock, also called Red Rock **Reservoir**.

Boating on West Okoboji Lake

Located south of Des Moines, it was completed in 1969 and has become a popular recreation area for people who live in the city. The next-largest reservoir is Rathbun Lake on the Chariton River.

CLIMATE

Iowa has hot, humid summers and cold, snowy winters. Winds often whip across the great open areas. In pioneer times, the prairie grasses would sometimes catch fire, and the ferocious winds would blow the fire across the land, devastating farms and settlements. Today, prairie fires can occur when grasses are dry. The winds can turn snowstorms into blinding blizzards. But the wind has some advantages, too. By 2008, more than 1,000 wind **turbines**—the third-highest number in the nation—were creating electricity in Iowa.

WORD TO KNOW

turbines *machines that make power by rotating blades driven by wind, water, or steam*

A tornado roars through Ames in November 2005.

Iowa is also prone to tornadoes. Tornadoes usually occur in the spring as cold, dry air from Canada meets warm, moist air from the Gulf of Mexico. When the two air masses meet, they may begin to spiral. Pockets of fast-spinning air may drop to the earth as tornadoes.

On average, Iowa experiences 49 twisters a year. The state's worst year on record for tornadoes was 2004, when 120 twisters touched ground, 57 in the month of May alone. Few of Iowa's tornadoes have been powerful enough to cause massive destruction. But in 1882, Grinnell was struck by two tornadoes at once, killing

Weather Report

This chart shows record temperatures (high and low) for the state, as well as average temperatures (July and January) and average annual precipitation.

Record high temperature . . . . 118°F (48°C) at Keokuk on July 20, 1934

Record low temperature . . . . –47°F (–44°C) at Washta on January 12, 1912, and at Elkader on February 3, 1996

Average July temperature, Des Moines . . . . 76°F (24°C)

Average January temperature, Des Moines. . . . . . . 23°F (–5°C)

Average annual precipitation, Des Moines . . . .36 inches (91 cm)

Source: National Climatic Data Center, NESDIS, NOAA, U.S. Department of Commerce

39 people. In 1976, a tornado destroyed every building in the town of Jordan. Fortunately, no one was killed. In 2008, the town of Parkersburg was destroyed by a tornado that whipped through with winds of more than 200 miles an hour (322 kph).

Iowa National Park Areas

This map shows some of Iowa's national parks, monuments, preserves, and other areas protected by the National Park Service.

Loess Hills in Five Ridge Prairie State Preserve

It takes 400 years for prairie grasses to produce 1 inch (2.5 centimeters) of new soil.

WORD TO KNOW

carbon *an element that plants need to grow*

THE GREAT PRAIRIE

When European settlers came to Iowa, about 85 percent of Iowa's land was tallgrass prairie. Today, less than one-tenth of 1 percent of that prairie grassland remains.

The most common prairie grasses in Iowa were big and little bluestem, Indian grass, switchgrass, and grama. Prairie grasses develop vast root systems that keep the plants alive during harsh winters, even when the part of the plant visible above ground appears to die back. Such grassland can also survive fire, which was once common on the open land.

Prairie grasses helped form Iowa's rich soil. Over the centuries, the roots and grasses gradually decayed. This process continually added **carbon** to the soil, producing the most fertile soil in the world.

Iowans are trying to save what prairie remains and restore some of what has been lost. The state's largest prairie preserve is Five Ridge Prairie near Sioux City. Hayden Prairie in northeast Iowa is the state's largest tract of prairie outside the Loess Hills. Neal Smith National Wildlife Refuge, established in 1990 in Jasper County, is a reconstructed (or replanted) tallgrass prairie.

When European settlers first arrived in Iowa, it was also covered by about 7 million acres (3 million hectares) of forest. Today, about one-third of that remains. Iowa produces high-quality oak and black walnut, which are used primarily in furniture making. Other hardwood trees found in upland areas are sugar maples, white ash, basswood, and serviceberry. Hardwoods that grow along rivers include sycamore, cottonwood, and silver maple. Conifers, or cone-bearing trees, grow naturally on some of the hills in northeastern Iowa.

PRAIRIE WILDLIFE

When Iowa was mostly tallgrass prairie, its largest animal was the American bison, or buffalo. These animals provided plenty of meat and other materials for the Native Americans who lived there. In the 19th century, European Americans killed nearly all of the bison. Today, some farmers are raising bison because the meat is much lower in fat than beef. A number of ranches in Iowa raise bison for meat production.

Otters and beavers once were found in huge numbers, especially around the wetlands. Now those wetlands are largely gone, and so are these mammals. A few black bears and mountain lions live in Iowa today, but the largest common mammal is the white-tailed deer.

Iowa is currently home to about 70 species of mammals, from little shrews to dog-sized coyotes. Muskrats

FAQ

Q8 WHY IS IOWA'S PRAIRIE CALLED TALLGRASS PRAIRIE?

A8 The prairie grasses were sometimes tall enough to hide a rider on horseback. Because more rain fell on the Iowa prairie than on the prairie land farther west, the grasses grew taller. The prairie to the west is called shortgrass prairie.

Bison

Bald eagles' nests are sometimes 5 feet (1.5 m) in diameter.

WORDS TO KNOW

endangered *in danger of becoming extinct throughout all or part of a range*

threatened *likely to become endangered in the foreseeable future*

Many bobcats make their home in Iowa forests.

and minks live in the wetlands, while bobcats prowl throughout the state. Opossums are found in woodlands and along waterways. The fox squirrel, which can grow up to 30 inches (76 cm) long, is the state's largest squirrel. The eastern cottontail and the white-tailed jackrabbit live side by side in the western part of the state.

As many as 400 species of birds pass through Iowa each year. Small birds include eastern goldfinches (the state bird), meadowlarks, bobolinks, and sparrows. Woodpeckers, owls, wrens, chickadees, and robins are common throughout the state. Millions of snow geese live at the DeSoto National Wildlife Refuge in western Iowa. Canada geese, tundra swans, and a variety of ducks are also found in Iowa.

Bald eagles were once **endangered**, but they have recently made a comeback. In Iowa, many bald eagles live

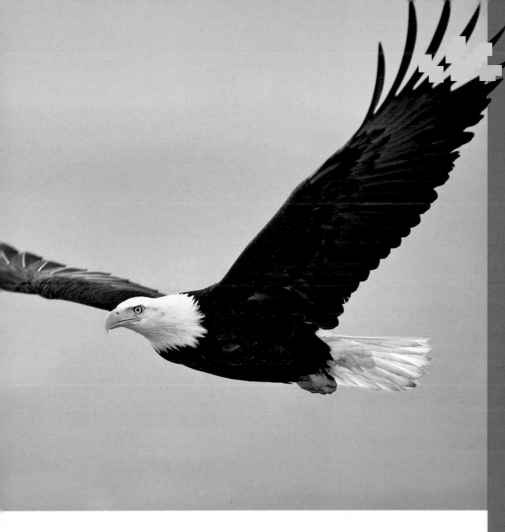

Bald eagles are making a comeback in Iowa.

ENDANGERED SPECIES

Several mammal species in Iowa are **threatened** or endangered, including the Indiana bat, which hibernates in caves, primarily in southern Iowa. Several birds in Iowa are also in danger of becoming extinct, including the piping plover and the least tern, both of which nest along rivers. Trumpeter swans are the largest waterfowl native to Iowa. In the 1800s, they nested in huge numbers in the prairie wetlands. But because of their beautiful feathers, they were hunted almost to extinction. Today, states are trying to reintroduce them to their former habitat. Several breeding pairs have now been released in Iowa. Some have settled at the Green Island State Wildlife Refuge on Sabula, an island in the Mississippi River.

Other endangered and threatened animals include the pallid sturgeon, which lives in the Missouri and Mississippi rivers, and the spotted skunk.

Trumpeter swan

at Lake Red Rock. The birds have also become increasingly common in and around Des Moines. Even if you don't spot the birds themselves, you can usually see their large nests atop tall trees.

PRESERVING THE LAND

Iowans have long been proud of how quickly they dug up the prairie and made the land productive. But in the early 20th century, they were already beginning to realize that perhaps they had done this too fast. Some of the original land needed to be conserved, and Iowans needed places for outdoor recreation. Thomas Macbride of the Iowa

JAY NORWOOD "DING" DARLING: THE DARLING OF DUCK STAMPS

The newspaper cartoons by Jay Norwood "Ding" Darling (1876–1962), especially in the *Des Moines Register and Leader*, got people talking about the damage Americans were doing to the environment. In 1934, he was appointed head of the U.S. Biological Survey. That same year, he developed the Federal Duck Stamp Program. This program, which is still active, requires waterfowl hunters to purchase a "duck stamp." The government uses the money from this tax to purchase and preserve critical wetlands. Darling was also a founder of the National Wildlife Federation.

? Want to know more? Visit www.factsfornow .scholastic.com and enter the keyword **Iowa**.

A stone lodge at Backbone State Park

Park and Forestry Association noted, "The prairies are plowed almost to the last acre; the woodlands have been cleared away entirely or converted into pasturelands." He pleaded for land conservation. So in 1920, the state created Iowa's first state park, Backbone, near Strawberry Point. The "backbone" is a ridge of rock.

The conservation movement grew, and Iowa became a leader in the movement to form state parks. Iowa's own "Ding" Darling became known nationwide for his work in encouraging conservation. A state park is named for him.

Nineteenth-century Iowa was a land of lakes, marshes, soggy prairies, and other wetlands. At that time, Iowa had more than 7 million acres (3 million ha) of wetlands. Today, the land has been drained, and less than 1 percent of the wetlands remain.

Wetlands are vital to animal life. They provide important feeding grounds for birds and other creatures. The more wetlands there are, the more kinds of plants and animals can live in an area. Many of the threatened or endangered species in Iowa live near wetlands. If more wetlands can be restored, the threat may be lessened.

Sometimes restoring wetlands requires nothing more than removing the drain tile in the ground. Other times, it involves installing systems to control the flow of water. Some Iowans have created wetlands where there once were none, for example on the sites of abandoned coal mines. Creating wetlands in these areas can gradually clean up the scarred land. One such site has become Banner Lakes at Summerset State Park, which opened in 2004. What had been Banner Pits, named for the massive pits where coal was dug, has become a major recreation area. The lakes that have formed are kept stocked with trout, to the delight of fishers—especially in winter when there are few places to fish.

MINI-BIO

ALDO LEOPOLD: RESTORING THE LAND

Aldo Leopold (1887–1948), a founder of the environmental movement, was born and raised in Burlington. He learned about the land and its plants from his father, a furniture maker who loved native plants. Determined to help save the natural world, Leopold became a forester. While working in Wisconsin, he spent weekends at the "Shack," a converted chicken coop on 120 acres (50 ha) of worn-out land along the Wisconsin River. It was here that he wrote A Sand County Almanac, a book filled with careful observation of the natural world and discussion of the need to respect the land. Leopold's book was one of the most influential books in the environmental movement.

 Want to know more? Visit www.factsfornow .scholastic.com and enter the keyword **Iowa.**

Early hunters attacking bison about 10,000 years ago

Woodland water jug

7500 BCE
Paleo-Indians live in what is now Iowa

7000 BCE
The Archaic culture develops

▲ **500 BCE**
Woodland Indian culture develops

CHAPTER TWO

FIRST PEOPLE

★

URING THE LAST ICE AGE, MUCH OF IOWA WAS COVERED BY A GLACIER. Until about 12,000 years ago, even the parts of the state that were not under ice were too cold for humans to live in. Perhaps people entered the area from the south in quest of mammoths and mastodons, but they did not stay until about 9,500 years ago. By then, the climate had warmed and forests covered the land.

Hopewell figurine

◄ **100** BCE
Hopewell culture emerges

650 CE
The Effigy Mounds are built

1600s
Ioways and other groups live in what is now Iowa

A mound in the forested Effigy
Mounds National Monument

Atlatl

EARLY PEOPLES

The first humans to live in Iowa are called Paleo-Indians (*paleo* means "ancient"). Working together, they hunted mastodons, mammoths, and giant versions of today's bison. They chipped stone to make weapons and tools that they used for cleaning their kill.

The Paleo-Indians were followed by peoples of the Archaic culture, which lasted from about 9,000 to 3,000 years ago. During this time, the climate grew warmer and drier, the forests gradually disappeared, and many large mammals died off. In what is now western Iowa, Archaic people began depending on bison for food. In eastern Iowa, they hunted deer and elk. They used a throwing stick called the atlatl, which enabled them to send spears longer distances and with greater force. The atlatl was good for killing animals on open land.

Archaic people developed sharp knives that they used to cut up the animals they hunted. They also used stones for grinding plant foods they found on their travels.

About 2,500 years ago, the Woodland Indian culture emerged. Woodland Indians lived a more settled existence than Archaic people. They built roundhouses from wood and mud, and made roofs of reeds and straw. They made clay pottery that they used to store water, vegetables, and seeds. Woodland peoples also began to hunt with bows and arrows. They cultivated grains that they found growing wild. Later Woodland Indians grew corn, which they learned about from people who lived farther south.

MOUND BUILDERS

Toward the end of the Woodland period, some people, especially in the Mississippi Valley, began to build large, permanent communities. This culture, which is called Hopewell—after the place in Ohio where the people were first identified—probably lasted from about 100 BCE to 700 CE.

Hopewell towns featured large, flat-topped mounds. Some of these mounds were used as burial sites, while others were used for religious ceremonies. Hopewells built the mounds by carrying thousands of baskets of soil to the site and forming it into shapes. Some of the mounds are in the shapes of animals.

WOW

In 1955, a girl from the small town of Turin discovered a site containing several skeletons thought to be at least 6,500 years old.

SEE IT HERE!

EFFIGY MOUNDS NATIONAL MONUMENT
The mounds that Native Americans of the Hopewell culture created for burying their people were sometimes made in the shapes of animals, called **effigies**. Within the 2,500-acre (1,000 ha) Effigy Mounds National Monument, located near McGregor in northeastern Iowa, are 206 mounds, 31 of them in the form of effigies. One of the biggest is the Great Bear Mound. It is 137 feet (42 m) long and 70 feet (21 m) across the shoulders of the bear's form. The mounds that are not effigies are mostly long or cone shaped. Although the effigy mounds were probably not built until about 650 CE, some of the other mounds may be almost 2,500 years old. Many of the mounds have floors sprinkled with iron oxide, which is also called red ochre, so the people who made them are sometimes called the Red Ochre Culture.

WORD TO KNOW

effigies *figures of people or animals*

Native American Peoples
(Before European Contact)

This map shows the general area of Native American peoples before European settlers arrived.

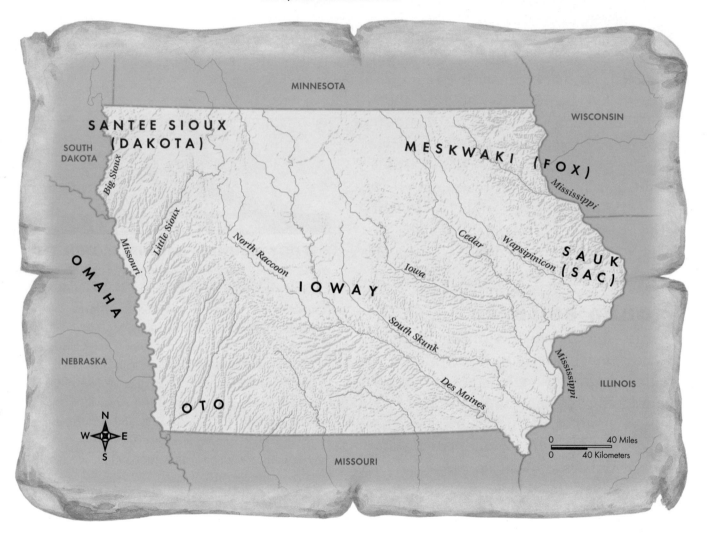

The Hopewell people were farmers. They grew corn, beans, and squash. They also traded widely, acquiring copper from people in today's Michigan and Minnesota, clamshells from the Mid-Atlantic region, and alligator teeth and skulls from Florida.

Mound builders gathering corn and squash

PLAINS VILLAGE PEOPLE

The Hopewell culture disappeared by 700. No one knows why. A new kind of culture gradually developed, called Oncota. Perhaps by 1200, people began living in villages, usually clustered along waterways.

In the western part of what is now Iowa, these people are called the Plains Village people. They were more common farther west in today's Nebraska and the Dakotas. They lived in villages with farmland spread out around them. They grew corn, which they dried and stored for long periods. For Plains Village people, growing crops became more important than hunting, though they did hunt bison.

In eastern Iowa, the Oneota people also lived in towns and grew crops in the surrounding fields. They fished and hunted in areas nearby. They traded widely with other peoples. In this way, they obtained copper. Oneota clay pots often included sparkling bits of clamshell acquired on trading trips.

The Oneota people probably gradually evolved into the Native American nations European explorers met in the 1600s. The largest of these groups was the Ioway Nation.

THE IOWAY NATION

Ioways believe that they split off from Ho-Chunks, or Winnebagos, people long ago when that group moved westward from Lake Michigan. These Wisconsin ancestors may have been Oneotas.

Though Ioways from Wisconsin had lived among dense forests, in Iowa they found prairie, with only a few trees. They soon changed their methods of growing crops and building houses to adapt to their new land. In the forests, they had built houses covered with bark. Now in Iowa, they covered bent branches with mats made from reeds. Ioway **artifacts** have been found throughout the state.

SHARING THE LAND

Over the years, many different Native groups traveled to Iowa. Some stayed for a time and then left. It's

Oneota pot

WORD TO KNOW

artifacts *items created by humans, usually for a practical purpose*

This drawing from the Meskwaki people illustrates their relationship to the natural world.

estimated that 17 different nations lived there at various times, including the Sauk, Meskwaki, Oto, Missouri, and Potawatomi peoples.

Ioways were generally tolerant of other Native peoples who entered their territory. In the mid-1600s, the Moingwena people lived at the mouth of a small river where it flowed into the Mississippi. They had probably been pushed across the Mississippi by attacks from the Iroquois people to the east, who were hunting for furs to trade with the French. It was there that Native people in Iowa first set eyes on Europeans.

READ ABOUT

The Marquette
and Jolliet
expedition, 1673

1673
*Jacques Marquette and
Louis Jolliet lead a party
into what is now Iowa*

1682 ▲
*René-Robert Cavelier,
Sieur de La Salle, claims
the Mississippi Valley,
including Iowa, for
France*

1788
*Julien Dubuque
becomes Iowa's
first permanent
European settler*

CHAPTER THREE

EXPLORATION AND SETTLEMENT

★

I T'S JUNE 1673. A group of explorers is paddling canoes down the Mississippi River. The leaders are Louis Jolliet, a Canadian-born adventurer, and Jacques Marquette, a French priest. On their eighth night in what would become Iowa, they camp at the mouth of a small river. Probably the Moingwena people, who live nearby, are keeping an eye on the strangers. But it isn't until that night that the two sets of people show themselves to one another.

1803

The United States buys the Louisiana Territory

◄ **1832**

Black Hawk and his Sauk followers resist being forced off their land

1833

European Americans are allowed to settle eastern Iowa

René-Robert Cavelier, Sieur de La Salle, traveling on the Mississippi River, 1682

FRENCH EXPLORATIONS

This first contact between Native people and Europeans in Iowa was brief. Marquette and Jolliet soon continued on their mission exploring the Mississippi River. When they traveled down it far enough to be certain that it emptied into the Gulf of Mexico, they turned around and went home.

A few years later, in 1682, René-Robert Cavelier, Sieur de La Salle, sailed farther than Marquette and Jolliet. When he reached the mouth of the Mississippi River, he claimed the entire river valley, including today's Iowa to the far north, for France. He named it Louisiana, after the French king Louis XIV.

French trappers soon ventured out across the vast land to acquire furs. The French founded New Orleans at the mouth of the Mississippi in 1718, but they did not explore or settle much of the vast territory.

European Exploration of Iowa

The colored arrows on this map show the routes taken by explorers between 1673 and 1820.

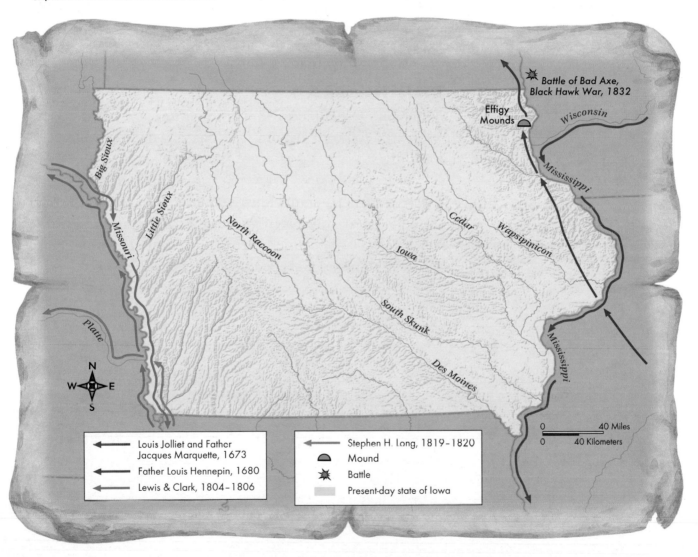

In 1754, France and Great Britain went to war over control of North America and the fur trade. When France was on the verge of losing what is known as the French and Indian War, it gave Spain the right to the land west of the Mississippi. Like France, Spain did little to settle or explore Louisiana, and French trappers continued to work in the region.

MINING LEAD

Some Native people in Iowa mined a black powder that they used for body decoration. The powder was galena, a lead ore.

Julien Dubuque, a French Canadian trader, became Iowa's first permanent European settler in 1788. He had initially been interested in trading for furs. After the Meskwaki people came to trust him, they told him about the galena mines. Europeans were eager to mine the lead

Julien Dubuque was buried in these cliffs along the Mississippi River, not far from the present-day city of Dubuque.

because it was used to make bullets. Meskwakis agreed that Dubuque could live on their land and mine the lead. He and the Meskwaki people worked together to profit from the lead mines, which he called Mines of Spain (*Las Minas Españolas*) because the Spanish claimed the territory at the time. The city of Dubuque now lies on that land.

THE LOUISIANA PURCHASE

By 1800, the Spanish were busy fighting a war in Europe, and they lost interest in their lands in North America. Spain traded the Louisiana region, including Iowa, back to the French. But soon the French also lost interest. Enslaved Africans in the French colony of Saint-Domingue (which became Haiti) rebelled. The successful uprising drained French resources, encouraging the French to give up on their colonies in the Americas.

By this time, the 13 British colonies along the Atlantic coast had fought for their independence and become the United States of America. U.S. president Thomas Jefferson wanted to buy the port of New Orleans to ensure that American ships had access to the Mississippi River, which was important for transporting goods to and from the nation's western regions. But in 1803, the French instead offered to sell both New Orleans and all of the Louisiana Territory to the United States for $15 million. It turned out to

Louisiana Purchase

This map shows the area (in yellow) that made up the Louisiana Purchase and the present-day state of Iowa (in orange).

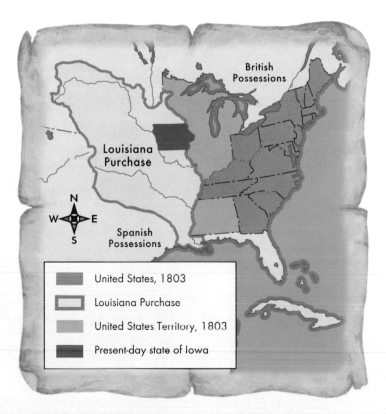

- United States, 1803
- Louisiana Purchase
- United States Territory, 1803
- Present-day state of Iowa

WOW

The Louisiana Purchase doubled the size of the United States at a cost of 4 cents an acre!

WORD TO KNOW

corps *a group working together on a special mission*

Meriwether Lewis and William Clark meeting with Native Americans

be one of the greatest land deals in history. Some or all of 15 states would eventually be carved from the territory, which stretched from the Mississippi River to the Rocky Mountains.

THE LEWIS AND CLARK EXPEDITION

Just what had the United States purchased? Jefferson decided that Americans needed to know more about the vast territory. He asked his personal secretary, Meriwether Lewis, to lead an expedition to explore the Louisiana Territory and beyond, all the way to the Pacific Ocean. Lewis asked an old army friend, William Clark, to join him. Lewis and Clark's **Corps** of Discovery included

Lewis and Clark endured difficult trails and bad weather during their journey.

MINI-BIO

YORK: THE FIRST AFRICAN IN IOWA

Probably the first person of African descent to enter Iowa was an enslaved African named York (c. 1770–c. 1831). A tall, agile, heavyset man, York accompanied the Lewis and Clark expedition to explore the land acquired through the Louisiana Purchase. Along with Sacagawea—a young Shoshone woman who joined the expedition in what is now North Dakota and served as interpreter—York served as a messenger of goodwill with the Native Americans. He was an expert hunter and fisherman and easily picked up new languages. After the expedition returned to St. Louis, York asked for his freedom. Years later, William Clark claimed he had freed York, but no one knows for certain.

Want to know more? Visit www.factsfornow.scholastic.com and enter the keyword **Iowa**.

more than 40 men, including York, an enslaved African who had been Clark's companion since childhood.

On May 14, 1804, the Corps of Discovery set out from St. Louis, Missouri, traveling up the Missouri River. Before they returned to St. Louis in September 1806, the group had traveled all the way to the Pacific Ocean and back. Along the way, they met many Native people, discovered new plants and animals, and mapped much of the land.

FIGHTING FOR THEIR LAND

At the time of the Louisiana Purchase, the Meskwaki people and their close allies, the Sauks, were living in southern Wisconsin, northern Illinois, and Iowa. In 1804, some

FAQ

Q: DID ANY MEMBERS OF THE CORPS OF DISCOVERY DIE ON THE JOURNEY?

A: Only one. Sergeant Charles Floyd died, probably of appendicitis, near what would become Sioux City, Iowa, on August 20, 1804.

The Sauk forces were defeated in the Black Hawk War of 1832.

WORD TO KNOW

ceding *giving up or granting*

Meskwaki and Sauk leaders signed a treaty **ceding** their lands east of the Mississippi River to the United States. But the people who lived in those lands knew nothing about the treaty and hadn't agreed to it. A Sauk named Black Hawk led those who opposed the treaty. In 1825 and 1830, Meskwaki and Sauk leaders signed additional agreements confirming that they would give up the land. At the same time, the U.S. government agreed to set aside land west of the Mississippi, in Iowa, for the Sauks and Meskwakis.

But Black Hawk was not willing to give up his homeland. In 1832, he led a group of Sauks, mostly old men, women, and children, back to the east bank of the Mississippi.

In the following months, U.S. troops tried to force them back west of the Mississippi in what is called the Black Hawk War. Many Sauks were killed, and Black Hawk surrendered on August 27.

The Sauks and Meskwakis were forced to cede a section of land in Iowa along the Mississippi. Called the Black Hawk Purchase, it was 40 to 50 miles (64 to 80 km) wide and was opened for settlement in June 1833.

OPEN FOR SETTLEMENT

That same month, hundreds of settlers crossed the Mississippi River to set up homes in the Black Hawk Purchase lands. These early settlers mainly came from states to the east such as Ohio, New York, and Virginia. Many of them moved west so they could obtain land. It was federal policy that land taken from Native Americans would be sold to settlers at a price of $100 for 80 acres (32 ha). Some men who served in the military received land rather than money.

It was hard work establishing a farm on the Iowa prairie. Most families had only the food and tools they brought with them. The tall grasses were difficult to cut, and their deep roots had to be dug out of the ground. Every member of the family had to help in order for fields

MINI-BIO

BLACK HAWK: FIGHTING FOR JUSTICE

Sauk leader Black Hawk (1767?–1838) grew up along the Mississippi River, hunting on land that later became part of the Louisiana Purchase. As more and more Europeans came into the area, he grew angry about the injustice of his people losing their land. Making up his mind to fight, he led hundreds of Native people from Iowa back into Illinois. The conflict that became known as the Black Hawk War lasted through the spring and summer of 1832, until Sauks and Meskwakis were overrun by U.S. troops at the Battle of Bad Axe in Wisconsin. Black Hawk was imprisoned until Sauks signed a treaty giving up their land.

? **Want to know more?** Visit www.factsfornow.scholastic.com and enter the keyword **Iowa**.

FAQ

Q: HOW DID IOWA GET ITS NICKNAME?

A: Some say Iowa is called the Hawkeye State as a tribute to Black Hawk. Others suggest that Iowa's leaders chose the nickname in honor of Hawkeye, the hero of James Fenimore Cooper's novel *The Last of the Mohicans*.

to be plowed and planted as soon as possible. Pioneers were able to break up and then plant only a few acres each summer.

If a family was lucky, someone nearby might start a church or perhaps a school that the children could attend when they didn't have too much work to do. Once in a while, neighbors gathered in one place for a celebration. And as more communities grew in Iowa, pioneers had more reason to celebrate.

THE HONEY WAR

When the Louisiana Territory was being split into future states, the border between Missouri and Iowa was very loosely described. Each would-be state eventu-

A school in Lincoln Township, mid-1800s

A sod house

ally claimed the same 2,600-square-mile (6,700 sq km) area near the Mississippi. In 1839, both Iowa and Missouri claimed taxes from the settlers in that area. When some Missourians cut down three honey trees (trees where honeybees had hives with large honey stocks), Iowans objected. Honey was as good as gold on the frontier, so the Iowans went to court. The event came to be called the Honey War when a journalist composed a song with the words:

Let the victor cut the trees
And have three bits in money,
And wear a crown from town to town,
Anointed in pure honey.

Not until 1851 did the U.S. Supreme Court establish the final boundary, drawing a line halfway between the possible borders.

Picture Yourself . . .

Building a Sod House

You've arrived in Iowa Territory and need a place to live. But there aren't any trees! The only building material you can find is the densely packed earth, or sod, in which the prairie grasses grow. You've heard that if it's cut into rectangles, sod can be stacked like bricks to form walls several feet thick. It's hard to cut the sod because the roots are tough. But you need a home, so you keep digging.

When you finally have enough sod bricks to begin building, you have to decide whether to leave spaces for windows. This would allow in light but also wind, which seems to always roar across the prairie. You need rugs to cover the earthen floor. But you probably can't do much about the insects that cling to the grass roots in the sod. When it rains, the soil might wash down on you, and if too much rain falls, the sod blocks will need to be replaced. There is no way to keep the house clean. No wonder you're glad when your family is finally able to build a house of wooden boards.

An advertisement
for land in Iowa and
Nebraska, mid-1800s

1846 ▶

*Iowa becomes the
29th state*

1857

*Meskwakis buy land
in north-central Iowa*

1858

*Iowa enacts a law
requiring that all
children be given a
free education*

CHAPTER FOUR

GROWTH AND CHANGE

★

SETTLER BY SETTLER, FARM BY FARM, EUROPEANS SPREAD ACROSS IOWA. Native Americans lost their land every step of the way. In 1837, the federal government forced the Sauk and Meskwaki peoples to cede land beyond the Black Hawk Purchase. By 1842, the United States owned almost one-third of Iowa.

1861–65
*Some 76,000 Iowans
fight in the Civil War*

1867 ▲
*The first railroad across
the state is completed*

1869
*Arabella Babb Mansfield
becomes the nation's first
female lawyer*

The Santee Sioux lost their remaining land in Iowa in 1851.

AWAY AND BACK AGAIN

Four years later, the Winnebago and Potawatomi people, whom the U.S. government had moved from Wisconsin to Iowa, had to give up their land in Iowa. They moved to Kansas and Minnesota. In 1845, Sauks and Meskwakis were forced to give up the last of their land in Iowa, and in 1851, the Santee (or Dakota) Sioux also lost their remaining Iowa lands.

These Native peoples were unhappy about losing their land, and the Meskwaki people hoped to buy theirs back. Some sold their own ponies to get cash and returned

Iowa: From Territory to Statehood

(1838–1846)

This map shows the original Iowa territory and the area (in yellow) that became the state of Iowa in 1846.

British Possessions

N
W　E
S

Lake Superior

MICHIGAN

Red

Missouri

Minnesota Territory, 1849

Wisconsin Territory, 1836

Mississippi

Lake Michigan

MICHIGAN 1837

Unorganized Territory

0　80 Miles
0　80 Kilometers

IOWA 1846

Missouri

Platte

ILLINOIS 1818

INDIANA 1816

MISSOURI 1821

KENTUCKY 1792

ARKANSAS 1836

TENNESSEE 1796

▢	Wisconsin Territory, 1836
▢	Iowa Territory, 1838
▢	State of Iowa, 1846
■	States
▨	U.S. territories
▢	British possessions

These Meskwakis established a
settlement in Tama in I857.

to Iowa in 1857. They found one white man willing to sell them land. Eventually, they came to own about 3,600 acres (1,450 ha) of fertile land. Today, they are the only government-recognized Native American nation in Iowa. Their land, in north-central Iowa, is not a reservation. It is called a settlement because Meskwakis bought it.

SETTLING A NEW STATE

In 1844, Iowa applied for statehood. The region's white population was 75,000 and growing rapidly. On December 28, 1846, Iowa became the nation's 29th state.

New settlers had poured into Iowa before it became a state. After it became a state, they came in even larger numbers. Between 1850 and 1900, the population of Iowa soared from 192,000 to 2,232,000. At the same time, Native people were being driven out of the area.

People from many different nations settled in Iowa, and their towns took on the character of the people who lived there. Dutch immigrants founded the town of Pella in 1847. In the 1850s, Decorah became the first Norwegian town west of the Mississippi. Czech and Danish communities were also established.

Germans had been among the new settlers who entered Iowa when the Black Hawk Purchase was opened for European settlement. For decades, most foreign-born people in the state were German. Many Germans settled in Dubuque to work the lead mines.

THE AMANA COLONIES

In 1855, German immigrants belonging to a church called the Community of True Inspiration started a group of small communities called the Amana Colonies. In the Amana villages, people shared everything, including work and its profits.

Many European settlers arrived in Iowa in the 1800s and built simple homes on acres of farmland.

FROM SLAVERY TO FREEDOM

Iowa was not yet a state when the territorial supreme court made a decision that struck a blow to slavery. An enslaved Missouri man named Ralph had been taken to Iowa to work in a Dubuque lead mine. But slavery was illegal in Iowa, and he began to work to earn his freedom. White **abolitionists** came to Ralph's aid when his owner demanded his return. The territorial supreme court ruled in 1839 that, having been allowed to go into Iowa as a free resident, Ralph was no longer enslaved.

Hundreds of enslaved people traveled through Iowa on the Underground Railroad, making their way to freedom.

WORD TO KNOW

abolitionists *people who work to end slavery*

AFRICAN AMERICANS IN IOWA

African Americans had lived in Iowa since before it became a state, but in small numbers. Some settled in Iowa to farm, hoping that it would be more welcoming than some other states. But this was not always the case. In 1839, Iowa passed a law designed to keep African migrants out of the state by requiring them to post a $500 bond. At the time, few people had $500. This law may not always have been enforced, but it discouraged the migrants from trying to enter the state. Then in the 1850s, the state legislature denied African Americans the right to vote, although it allowed them to testify in court.

Black pioneers sought the same rights as other Americans in Iowa. They were aided by white people who opposed slavery and unfair laws.

MINI-BIO

CHARLOTTA PYLES: FREEDOM FIGHTER OF KEOKUK

Charlotta Pyles (1806–1880) was born into slavery in Kentucky. She married a free black man, and they had 12 children. When her owner died in the early 1850s, his daughter freed Charlotta and helped her and her family move from Kentucky to Keokuk, Iowa. Charlotta soon began trying to raise money to buy her two sons-in-law, who had been left behind in Kentucky. She traveled to the East, where abolitionist groups paid her to give speeches against slavery. Drawing large audiences, she raised the $3,000 she needed. She and her husband also turned their home into a station on the Underground Railroad.

? **Want to know more?** Visit www.factsfornow .scholastic.com and enter the keyword **Iowa**.

In southern Iowa, African Americans and whites began working with the Underground Railroad, a network of safe places where people could get help as they fled slavery. Because of its location in the center of the country, the state was an important part of the journey for those heading to Canada to escape slavery in the South. Most entered Iowa from Missouri and Nebraska and traveled up the Mississippi River to Illinois. Des Moines, Grinnell, Iowa City, Tipton, and Clinton all had stops on the Underground Railroad. It's estimated that more than 1,000 runaway slaves made their way through Iowa.

THE CIVIL WAR

Throughout the 1850s, tension grew between Northern and Southern states over the issue of slavery. Some Northerners, including many in Iowa, wanted to abolish, or end, slavery. Many others simply wanted to limit its expansion into new territories. In 1860, Abraham Lincoln was elected president. Many Southerners

WORKING ON THE UNDERGROUND RAILROAD

The town of Low Moor in southeastern Iowa was on the Underground Railroad path followed by people fleeing slavery. In Low Moor, G. W. Weston, an abolitionist, communicated with other abolitionists in code. He sent the following letter to C. B. Campbell, giving notice that two people fleeing slavery were on their way:

Low Moor, May 6, 1859.

Mr. C. B. C.:

Dear Sir—By tomorrow evening's mail, you will receive two volumes of the "Irrepressible Conflict" bound in black. After perusal, please forward, and oblige.

Yours truly, G. W. W.

The First Iowa Regiment fighting at the Battle of Wilson's Creek, near Springfield, Missouri, August 1861

WORD TO KNOW

seceded *withdrew from an association*

feared that he would abolish slavery. In the following months, 11 Southern states **seceded** from the Union and formed a new nation called the Confederate States of America. Lincoln was prepared to fight to preserve the Union, and in April 1861, the Civil War began.

No battles were fought in Iowa, but 76,000 Iowans fought in the war, including one regiment of black soldiers. Iowan troops became the first white soldiers to fight alongside African American troops. This occurred at the Battle of Milliken's Bend in Louisiana, on June 7, 1863. By the time the Union won the Civil War in 1865, more than 13,000 soldiers from Iowa had given their lives.

THE QUEST FOR EQUAL RIGHTS

In 1858, the Iowa legislature passed a law requiring that all children in Iowa be provided with a free education. However, Iowa's public schools were racially **segregated**.

Alexander Clark of Muscatine wanted his daughter Susan to study English grammar, but her all-black school did not offer that subject in 1867. Hoping to get Susan into the all-white school, Clark took his case to court, and the Iowa Supreme Court ruled that she should be allowed to attend the all-white school. It concluded that keeping her out of the white school would "tend to perpetuate the national differences of our people and stimulate a constant **strife**, if not war, of races." It wasn't for another 86 years that the U.S. Supreme Court ruled that the separation of races in schools went against the Constitution.

GROWING BUSINESSES

Steamboats had transported goods to Iowans since 1823. Boats traveled up and down the Mississippi and Missouri rivers along the border as well as some other rivers such as the Des Moines. If towns could not be reached by river, stagecoaches were used, but bad weather could bring stagecoach travel to a halt.

MINI-BIO

ALEXANDER CLARK: SEEKING EQUALITY

Perhaps no figure in Iowa was more devoted to equality and justice than Alexander Clark (1826–1891), who arrived from Ohio as a teenager in the 1840s. He opened a barbershop and eventually became one of the wealthiest African Americans in Muscatine. Clark was instrumental in having the state constitution changed so that the word white no longer was used to describe who could vote. He also launched campaigns to end laws that **discriminated** against African Americans and recruited more than 1,000 African Americans for the Union cause. In 1890, he was named U.S. **ambassador** to Liberia.

? **Want to know more?** Visit www.factsfornow .scholastic.com and enter the keyword **Iowa**.

WORDS TO KNOW

segregated *separated from others, according to race, class, ethnic group, religion, or other factors*

strife *bitter disagreement*

discriminated *treated unequally based on race, gender, religion, or other factors*

ambassador *the chief representative of a government in another country*

Workers building tracks for the Sante Fe Railway Company, near Fort Madison, January 1887

WORD TO KNOW

transcontinental *crossing an entire continent*

The first transcontinental railroad was completed in 1869, but a bridge wasn't built across the Missouri River at Council Bluffs until 1872. Until then, ferries had to take passengers and cargo across the river.

Railroads solved this problem. In 1862, President Abraham Lincoln authorized a **transcontinental** railroad. At this time, most of the eastern portion of the railroad was already completed. The western part was to start at Council Bluffs on the Missouri River on Iowa's western border. A train roared across Iowa for the first time in 1867. Soon there were five lines across the state, and most towns were near a railway depot.

The government gave railroads large tracts of land in exchange for laying tracks through the state, and many settlers bought this land from the railroads. The first railroads in Iowa went through existing towns, but after the track reached the center of the state, there were few towns, and the railroad companies had to create them. This speeded settlement of the state.

Once the rail lines were finished, Iowa's agricultural land became a major source of grains for the country. These crops were shipped through Chicago, Illinois, to markets in the East.

Iowa became a meatpacking center, where countless hogs were butchered. Several Chicago meatpacking businesses built plants in Iowa, especially around Sioux City. The more corn Iowa grew, the more hogs could be fed. And once railroads introduced refrigerated cars, the meat could be shipped fresh. Iowa became the biggest meat-producing state in the country.

In addition, the timber industry in Iowa boomed in the second half of the 1800s. Between 1850 and 1890, millions of logs were sent downriver from Minnesota and Wisconsin for milling in Iowa sawmills.

Many coal mines also opened in Iowa. The railroads depended on coal to generate the steam that made their engines run, so coal was mined wherever it was found. "Coal towns" were quickly built and just as quickly torn down when the coal ran out. At one time, about 400 coal mines were active in the state.

Many African Americans came to Iowa to work in coal mines after the Civil War. Others found work in

KATE SHELLEY: YOUNG HEROINE

On a stormy night in 1881, 16-year-old Kate Shelley (1865–1912) of Moingona saw that heavy rain had washed out the wooden support for the railway near her home. One locomotive had already fallen into the gap, killing two crewmen. Knowing that a passenger train was about to come through, Shelley began crawling in the driving wind and rain along the tracks that crossed a bridge more than 600 feet (183 m) long. Water was almost up to the tracks. When she reached solid land again, she was still carrying her lantern and was able to signal the engineer of the oncoming train in time to stop it. Her brave deed saved many lives. When a new bridge was built across the Des Moines River in 1901, it was named the Kate Shelley High Bridge. The depot where she later worked became the Kate Shelley Railroad Museum and Park.

? Want to know more? Visit www.factsfornow .scholastic.com and enter the keyword **Iowa**.

Jesse and Frank James and their gang of outlaws robbed their first train on July 21, 1873, near Adair.

SEE IT HERE!

OLD CAPITOL MUSEUM

The Old Capitol Museum in Iowa City features pages from the carefully preserved diaries of Iowa youngsters and young adults including an elementary school student, a Meskwaki child, and a Civil War soldier. This enables visitors to find out what life was like during the 1800s through the eyes of the people who lived then. For example, Mary Griffith, who lived in western Iowa, wrote: "April 29, 1880: Very windy. The scarlet fever casts a gloom over the whole City. Three funerals this afternoon. Mrs. Davis and another one of the children were buried. That makes four out of that family in five days."

Iowa's larger cities. From 1900 to 1922, the majority of the people in the coal town of Buxton were African American. The residents soon created a library, a literary society, and a YMCA, and its black and white citizens—including many Swede, Slovak, and Welsh immigrants—all enjoyed these facilities.

WOMEN'S RIGHTS

During the Civil War, many male teachers went off to fight, and women took their places in the classroom. Many women also served as nurses during the war,

A mining village in Zenorsville, near Gilbert, around 1890

These women attended a women's rights convention in Oskaloosa in 1889.

while at home women began breaking into new professions.

Lucy Hobbs Taylor studied dentistry as a private pupil and then began to practice in Iowa, in both Bellevue and McGregor. In 1865, she was admitted as a senior-level student at the Ohio College of Dental Surgery and earned her degree, becoming the first fully trained female dentist in the world. Arabella Babb Mansfield,

GROUNDBREAKING LAWYER

Arabella Babb Mansfield (1846–1911), the daughter of Burlington farmers, graduated from Iowa Wesleyan University in Mount Pleasant, where she later taught. She and her husband both began to study law, and they applied together to be admitted to the bar (meaning they would officially be allowed to practice law). The judge handling her bar decided that the words *men* and *male* in the law could be applied to women. She was admitted to the Iowa bar in 1869, making her the first woman lawyer in the United States. Mansfield never actually practiced law, but she encouraged other women to leap into an area that had previously been only for men.

Amelia Bloomer wearing the trousers she made famous

a native of Burlington, became the nation's first female lawyer.

Some Iowa women worked to change life for all women. Council Bluffs resident Amelia Bloomer worked to gain women the right to vote. She was also the first woman to own, operate, and edit a newspaper for women. It was called *The Lily: A Ladies' Journal*. Today, Bloomer is best remembered for a type of clothing called bloomers—loose trousers gathered at the ankle. Amelia Bloomer didn't design the bloomers. Instead, they came to be called bloomers after she wrote a newspaper article about how comfortable they were.

ENGLAND IN AMERICA

The British had been coming to Iowa for decades. By 1850, probably about half of the Iowans born outside the United States were British. In 1877, three English brothers with the last name Close started buying land in lightly settled areas in the western part of the state, centered at Le Mars. They invited young English gentlemen to join them and become farmers.

Hundreds of English families took advantage of the new land. Even wealthy people bought land.

Many of them came just for fun, turning towns into sports centers. They hunted foxes, danced at fancy balls, and raced horses. But by 1900, these wealthy English people had sold their land and gone elsewhere.

Most Iowans, however, had come to stay. They were building homes and businesses, ready to face the 20th century.

Storefronts in Rutland, 1906

BUFFALO BILL CODY: LEGEND OF THE OLD WEST

Iowa wasn't yet a state when "Buffalo Bill" Cody (1846–1917) was born near Le Claire. He earned his nickname working as a hunter supplying the railroads with buffalo meat, and he later worked as an army scout. Interest in the Wild West ran high in the late 1800s, and in 1883, Cody founded Buffalo Bill's Wild West, a show that included shooting exhibitions, bareback riding, and reenactments of historic events. Later, Buffalo Bill helped found the city of Cody, Wyoming. He also wrote a book about his exploits called Buffalo Bill's Own Story, but it's not certain how much of it was true.

? **Want to know more?** Visit www.factsfornow .scholastic.com and enter the keyword **Iowa**.

READ ABOUT

A view of Main
Street in Dubuque,
early 1900s

1922 ▲
May E. Francis becomes
the first woman elected to
statewide office in Iowa

1930s
The Rural Electrification
Program brings electricity
to Iowa farms

1942
The Women's Army
Auxiliary Corps is
established at Fort
Des Moines

CHAPTER FIVE

MORE MODERN TIMES

★

B Y 1900, SO MANY PEOPLE HAD MOVED INTO IOWA AND CLEARED LAND FOR FARMING THAT THE PRAIRIE WAS GONE. Most Iowans lived on farms. The state also had many small towns, which provided supplies for the farms. The farmers traveled to these towns on horseback or with wagons. The coming of the automobile would bring Iowans closer to one another.

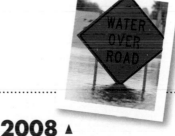

1980s
*Many Iowa
farms fail*

2002
*Iowa makes
English the state's
official language*

2008 ▲
*A great flood
devastates Iowa*

2012
*Drought destroys
crops and kills
fish across Iowa*

Soldiers at Camp Dodge, 1918

WORLD WAR I

In 1914, World War I began in Europe. During this war, the Allies, which were led by Great Britain and France, fought the Central powers, which were led by Germany and Austria-Hungary. During the war, the first African American officers in the U.S. Army were trained at the Fort Des Moines Provisional Army Officer Training School. World War I ended in 1918 after the United States came to the aid of the Allies and helped defeat the Central powers.

Many Iowans were of German heritage, and life was sometimes difficult for them during the war. Some people stopped speaking German because they feared their neighbors would think they were disloyal to the United States. Some Iowa towns even went so far as to change their German-sounding names. Germania, for example, became Lakota. Schools stopped offering courses in the German language.

BETWEEN THE WARS

In 1916, the Iowa legislature put a woman **suffrage** amendment before the public, but Iowans failed to approve it. The efforts of women all over the United States finally paid off in 1920 when Congress passed the 19th Amendment, giving women the right to vote. Then in 1922, May E. Francis was elected state superintendent of public instruction, making her the first woman in Iowa to gain elective office.

During the 1920s, Americans were eager to put the war behind them. It was the Roaring Twenties, a time when people went to the movies and danced to jazz music floating out of their radios. More Iowans bought cars, helping to reduce the isolation of farm families. With more cars, Iowa began improving its roads. The improved roads allowed children to attend school in neighboring towns.

THE GREAT DEPRESSION

Beneath all the energy of the Roaring Twenties, the economy was not strong. By 1929, the United States and the world had fallen into a severe economic downturn called the Great Depression. Businesses failed. Factories let their workers go. Individuals and businesses couldn't repay their loans, so banks went out

MINI-BIO

CARRIE CHAPMAN CATT: VOTES FOR WOMEN!

Iowan Carrie Chapman Catt (1859–1947) was one of the leaders of the fight to gain woman suffrage. Born in Wisconsin, she grew up in Charles City, Iowa, and graduated from Iowa State University. She served as superintendent of schools in Mason City and later began to concentrate on her fight for voting rights. During the next 20 years, she mobilized more than a million women and men to work for women's right to vote. After they were successful in getting the Nineteenth Amendment passed, Catt founded the League of Women Voters. Her childhood home in Charles City is a museum.

❓ **Want to know more?** Visit www.factsfornow.scholastic.com and enter the keyword **Iowa**.

WORD TO KNOW

suffrage *the right to vote*

The dining hall at a Civilian Conservation Corps program in Hampton, 1936

of business. Some people who had put their life savings in banks lost their money.

Without money, people couldn't buy food from farmers, so farmers suffered. Iowa farmers had their own food to eat, but they couldn't sell their crops. To make matters worse, a terrible drought struck the Great Plains, which stretched into western Iowa. The fertile topsoil dried up and blew away in the wind. The clouds of dust sometimes darkened skies as far away as the East Coast.

The federal government started programs in the 1930s to put people back to work. In Iowa, young men hired by the Civilian Conservation Corps built dams and improved parks. The government also provided electricity to many rural areas for the first time. Until this program, called Rural Electrification, was started, few Iowa farms had electricity.

WORLD WAR II

World War II began in Europe in 1939 when Germany invaded Poland. Great Britain and France came to Poland's defense, and soon war raged across the continent.

Many Americans wanted the United States to stay out of the war, but after Japan, an ally of Germany, bombed a U.S. naval base at Pearl Harbor, Hawai'i, on December 7, 1941, the United States entered the war. Eventually, more than 276,000 Iowans served in the war. About 8,400 of them died.

Frank Sanache (right), seen here with his brother, Willard, joined the U.S. Army in January 1941, along with 26 other Meskwakis.

THE FIGHTING SULLIVANS

Everyone in Waterloo knew the Sullivan brothers. There were five of them—George, Frank, Joe, Matt, and Leo—all close in age. When a friend died in the attack on Pearl Harbor, the three younger Sullivans decided to join the two older brothers, who were already serving in the U.S. Navy. The brothers insisted on serving together. The Navy agreed and assigned all five to the USS *Juneau*. In a battle in November 1942 in the Pacific Ocean, the *Juneau* took a direct torpedo hit and sank. All five Sullivan brothers died. The Navy has never again allowed so many members of one family to serve together.

A Women's Army Auxiliary Corps battalion at Fort Des Moines, 1942

FAQ

Q8 DID THE WAR EVER COME TO IOWA?

A8 In the late 1940s, the Japanese sent bomb-carrying balloons up into westerly winds, hoping that the bombs would set American forests on fire. One balloon reached Iowa before landing in a field, but nothing was set afire.

The war brought the Great Depression to an end. Industry picked up because the military needed supplies. The war also increased demand for Iowa farm products.

Women had served in the military as nurses in earlier conflicts, but in World War II, women took on broader roles. Iowa served as the training ground for the first units of women to serve. In 1942, the Women's Army Auxiliary Corps (WAAC) was established at Fort Des Moines. The next year, the U.S. Navy created a training school for women on the campus of Iowa State Teachers College in Cedar Falls. The first 1,500 members of the Women Appointed for Voluntary Emergency Service (WAVES) came from all over the country.

Clarinda and Algona were the sites of prisoner of war camps. The first German POWs arrived in the spring of 1944. In all, more than 10,000 Germans were held in Iowa, either at the main camps or branch camps. The branch camps were run by companies that employed the prisoners, who detasseled corn, cut timber, and worked in food-processing plants. Prisoners from Italy and Japan were also held in Iowa.

LEAVING THE FARM

In the middle of the century, Iowa's rural population was declining. Although Iowa farms remained very productive, they were using more machinery and thus required fewer workers. By 1940, only 57 percent of Iowans lived in rural areas.

During the 1970s, many Iowa farmers bought expensive new machinery because they were getting high prices for their crops overseas. But during the 1980s, crop prices fell. Farmers could not repay their loans, and many went out of business. As Iowa's farms failed, many of its businesses that supplied farmers also suffered. John Deere, a company that makes tractors and other farm machines, laid off thousands of workers in several Iowa cities.

From 1970 to 2000, the nation's population grew about 40 percent, but Iowa's population grew only 5 percent, and one-third of its counties—all rural—lost population. People were leaving their family farms and moving to the city or out of state. The loss of population was hard on those who remained. When the population of a county

KHRUSHCHEV COMES TO IOWA

Following World War II, the United States and the **Soviet Union**, which had been allies during World War II, became bitter rivals. They entered a long period called the Cold War, during which they vied for power around the world.

Iowa farmer Roswell Garst believed that lasting peace could be achieved by sharing agricultural technology and encouraging the Soviet Union to produce more food to feed its hungry people. He invited Soviet leader Nikita Khrushchev to his farm at Coon Rapids. Garst was surprised when Khrushchev accepted his invitation. Iowa National Guardsmen lined the highways leading up to the farm when Khrushchev came on September 23, 1959. Garst told Khrushchev, "We two farmers could settle the problems of the world faster than diplomats."

WORD TO KNOW

Soviet Union *a large nation in eastern Europe and northern and central Asia that formed in 1922 and split apart into Russia and several smaller republics in 1991*

PEACE AND
AGRICULTURE
S ASSOCIATION

SAVE
OUR
FARMS

PARIT
OT

PARITY

SAVE THE
FARM
for

Farmers and their supporters at a rally at the state capitol, 1983

MINI-BIO

NORMAN BORLAUG: FEEDING THE HUNGRY

Norman Borlaug (1914–2009) grew up working on his family farm in Iowa. As an adult, he became a scientist who worked to develop crops that would resist disease and not require the use of expensive chemicals. The new types of corn he developed increased food supplies in countries around the world. His role in what was called the Green Revolution earned him the 1970 Nobel Peace Prize. In 1997, a writer in the *Atlantic Monthly* said that, because of his achievements in preventing hunger, Borlaug "saved more lives than any other person who has ever lived."

? **Want to know more?** Visit www.factsfornow .scholastic.com and enter the keyword **Iowa**.

shrinks, fewer taxes are collected. So the services that a government provides—such as road upkeep, fire and police protection, maintaining schools—also shrink.

In 1985, legislators approved the formation of a state lottery as a way of raising money. By 2008, Iowa had earned more than $1.1 billion in profits from the lottery.

NEW ARRIVALS

Although many Iowans were leaving the state in the late 20th century, other people were moving to Iowa to start new lives. In the 1970s, church groups and other organizations in the state began to settle refugees from war in Southeast Asia. During this time, many families from Vietnam and Laos settled in Iowa. Many Iowa cities have seen an influx of immigrants from China, Japan, and Middle Eastern countries. In recent decades, large numbers of Latinos have also moved to Iowa. Many work for Iowa's meatpacking plants, bakeries, farms, and a host of other businesses.

A baker in Marshalltown, 2007

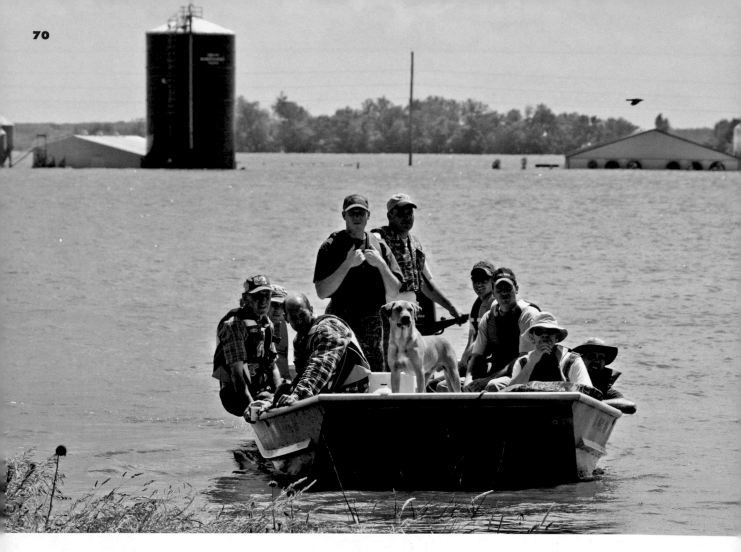

Residents navigating the streets of Oakville during the 2008 flood

WORD TO KNOW

levees *human-made wall-like embankments, often made of earth, built along a river to prevent flooding*

21ST-CENTURY DISASTERS

The first six months of 2008 were the wettest in Iowa's recorded history, with almost 2 feet (0.6 m) of rainfall. Cedar Rapids, Iowa City, Des Moines, and hundreds of small towns were flooded, with filthy water standing for weeks in houses, stores, schools, and fields. Bridges along the Mississippi were closed as **levees** collapsed, loosing the river onto the land.

Just as Iowans were recovering from the devastating floods of 2008, disaster struck again. On July 24, 2010, the Delhi Dam in the eastern part of the state failed after 10 inches (25 cm) of rain fell in just 12 hours. Water poured over the dam and rushed into downstream towns, which had to be evacuated. In 2012, the state began a $12-million reconstruction project on the damaged dam.

In the summer of 2012, Iowans faced their worst drought in nearly 50 years. Iowa's corn and soybean crops were devastated, causing food prices to rise around the world. Record-high temperatures dried up rivers, killing tens of thousands of fish throughout the Midwest. Some experts estimated that losses to the fishing industry could amount to hundreds of millions of dollars. In late 2013, farmers were still facing unusually dry conditions throughout most of the region. Through the years, Iowans have had to deal with many hardships, and they remain resilient.

The Des Moines skyline

READ ABOUT

Fans cheer for the
University of Iowa
football team at
a 2012 game.

CHAPTER SIX

PEOPLE

★

IOWANS ARE PROUD OF THEIR NATIVE HERITAGE. And they embrace new-comers to their state. They also are proud of how their pioneer ancestors turned the open prairie into farmland and made a home for themselves. The pioneers who settled Iowa had to be tough and hardworking to survive. They also had to be friendly. Since the nearest family lived far away, they were happy to see each other and always ready to lend a hand. Iowans' reputation for friendliness lives on to this day.

Iowa Population Growth

This chart shows Iowa's population changes between 1840 and 2010.

Source: U.S. Census Bureau, 2010 census

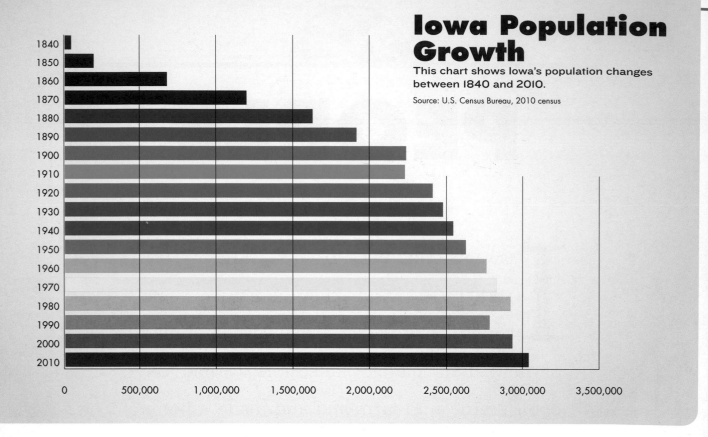

Year	
1840	
1850	
1860	
1870	
1880	
1890	
1900	
1910	
1920	
1930	
1940	
1950	
1960	
1970	
1980	
1990	
2000	
2010	

0   500,000   1,000,000   1,500,000   2,000,000   2,500,000   3,000,000   3,500,000

CITY AND COUNTRY

There's no such thing as a really big city in Iowa. In 2010, Iowa had 55 people per square mile (21 per sq km). Neighboring Illinois, in contrast, had 231 people per square mile (89 per sq km) in 2010. Well more than half of Iowans live in cities and their suburbs.

Iowa had more towns in the past than it does now. Many towns have disappeared from the map. Most often, this happened when a railroad came through the area but did not pass through the towns. Without railroad service, the towns withered. People moved away, and gradually the abandoned buildings fell down. Some river towns were abandoned because the rivers flooded too frequently. And many Iowa coal towns disappeared after the coal ran out.

Where Iowans Live

The colors on this map indicate population density throughout the state.
The darker the color, the more people live there.

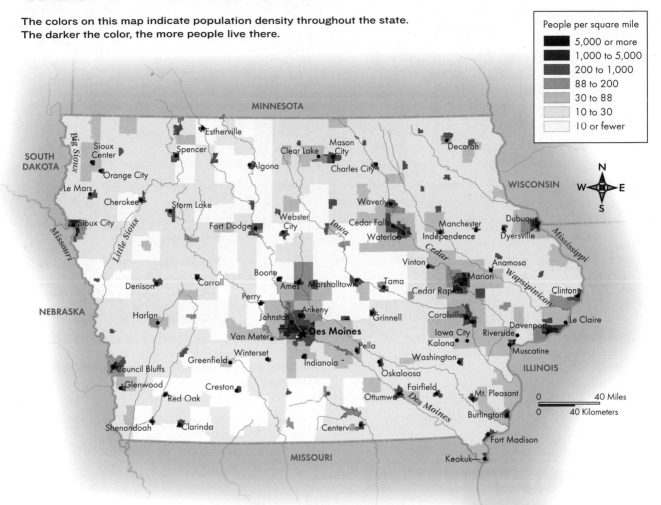

People per square mile

■	5,000 or more
■	1,000 to 5,000
■	200 to 1,000
■	88 to 200
■	30 to 88
■	10 to 30
□	10 or fewer

THE PEOPLE OF IOWA

Between 1850 and 1860, Iowa's population tripled. Some of the Iowans came from states to the east, while others came from Europe. Many German, Irish, Swedish, and Dutch people moved to Iowa. Elk Horn and Kimballton were home to the largest rural Danish settlements in the nation. Even today, most Iowans are of German or Irish descent.

Big City Life

This list shows the population of Iowa's biggest cities.

City	Population
Des Moines	203,433
Cedar Rapids	126,326
Davenport	99,685
Sioux City	82,684
Waterloo	68,406

Source: U.S. Census Bureau, 2010 census

The ribbon-cutting ceremony for a community center in Dubuque

SEE IT HERE!

KALONA'S AMISH

Near Kalona is the largest community of Amish people west of the Mississippi. The Amish are a strict religious group of Swiss-German descent. The Amish believe in living simply. They drive horse-drawn buggies rather than cars. They do not use electricity or have telephones in their homes. The Amish value their traditional skills and crafts, and many Amish women are accomplished quilters. The town of Kalona is home to the Quilt and Textile Museum, and the Amish hold a huge quilt show each April.

Today, Iowa's immigrant population is growing by leaps and bounds. The Asian population is growing faster than any other group. Most Asians in Iowa are of Vietnamese, Indian, or Chinese heritage. From 2010 to 2012, the number of Asians increased by nearly 11 percent, and Asians now account for almost 2 percent of the state's total population.

Many immigrants to Iowa are of Hispanic, or Latino, heritage. Many come from Mexico, El Salvador, and Colombia. Between 2000 and 2012, the Latino population increased by nearly 96 percent, making Latinos the state's second-largest ethnic group. An estimated 24,000 Latinos live in the Des Moines area. All over Iowa, Latinos have opened small businesses. In 2007, there were nearly 2,500 Latino-owned businesses in the state.

About 4 percent of the people in Iowa were born in other countries. In the 1990s, many immigrants from Bosnia settled in Waterloo as they fled their war-torn nation. In the first decade of the 21st century, immigrants from Myanmar, formerly known as Burma, came to Iowa. Today, more than 800 Burmese live in the Cedar Valley between Iowa City and Davenport. They, too, have come to escape civil war, and they are attracted by the promise of jobs, good schools, and religious freedom. In the town of Columbus Junction, many Burmese immigrants are finding jobs in meatpacking plants. Some newcomers are opening up small businesses.

African Americans have lived in Iowa since the first non-Native settlers entered the region. Today, most of Iowa's African Americans live in cities, particularly Des

MINI-BIO

TOMÁS RIVERA: EDUCATOR

Tomás Rivera (1935–1984) was the son of migrant workers who traveled each year from Texas to Iowa to harvest crops. His grandfather often told him stories and encouraged him to discover even more stories by going to the library. The joy of reading turned Rivera into a novelist, educator, and the first minority chancellor in the University of California system. The story of his discovery of the library was told by Pat Mora in the book *Tomás and the Library Lady*.

? Want to know more? Visit www.factsfornow.scholastic.com and enter the keyword **Iowa**.

People QuickFacts

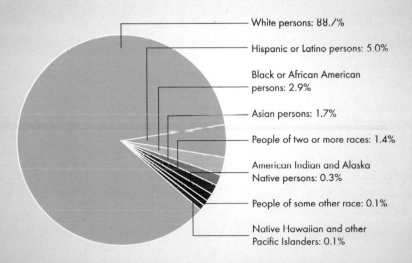

- White persons: 88.7%
- Hispanic or Latino persons: 5.0%
- Black or African American persons: 2.9%
- Asian persons: 1.7%
- People of two or more races: 1.4%
- American Indian and Alaska Native persons: 0.3%
- People of some other race: 0.1%
- Native Hawaiian and other Pacific Islanders: 0.1%

Source: U.S. Census Bureau, 2010 census

Moines. Native Americans make up about 0.3 percent of the state's population. Some live on Meskwaki land, while others live in cities. The Meskwaki people are encouraging young people to learn the Meskwaki language.

EDUCATION

Until about 1920, most Iowa children outside cities walked to a nearby one-room schoolhouse for their education. There were thousands of such schools throughout the state. Usually, one teacher taught all children up through eighth grade. Gradually the one-room schools were closed, and rural children were bused into the nearest towns for school. Today, Iowa has one of the highest graduation rates in the country.

WOW

The world's first automatic electronic digital computer was built in the physics building at Iowa State College in Ames in 1939. Called the Atanasoff-Berry Computer, or ABC, it was built by a physics professor, John Atanasoff, and a graduate student, Clifford Berry.

Students on the Iowa State University campus

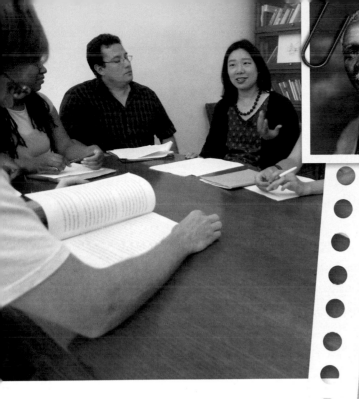

Participants in the Iowa Writers' Workshop

GEORGE WASHINGTON CARVER: INNOVATIVE BOTANIST

George Washington Carver (c. 1861–1943) was born in Missouri to an enslaved woman. As an adult, Carver enrolled in Simpson College in Indianola, Iowa. He transferred to Iowa State, becoming the school's first black student and later its first black teacher. He became a respected **botanist**. In 1896, he began working at Alabama's Tuskegee Institute, a school for African Americans. There he became focused on the challenge of helping poor farmers make a living. He tested alternating the planting of cotton with peanuts, which replenished the nutrients in the soil. This led to numerous discoveries about uses of peanuts and sweet potatoes, as well as ways to fertilize soil.

? Want to know more? Visit www.factsfornow.scholastic.com and enter the keyword **Iowa**.

Iowa City is home to the University of Iowa, the state's largest college. In 1855, it became the first public university in the nation to admit women on an equal basis with men. Today, it has more than 31,000 students. The school is the site of the Iowa Writers' Workshop, where many leading writers have taught or studied. At least 17 poets, novelists, and journalists who have attended the workshop or taught there have won Pulitzer Prizes.

Another state-supported university, Iowa State University in Ames was long called the Iowa State College of Agriculture and Mechanic Arts. Today, it is still known for its science and agriculture programs. Grinnell College, a highly regarded small college, is located in the town of Grinnell.

WORD TO KNOW

botanist *a scientist who studies plants*

HOW TO TALK LIKE AN IOWAN

Want to fit in in Iowa? Here are a few terms you should know:

- *Hogwash*—nonsense!
- *Uff dah!*—in Decorah and other Norwegian communities, it can mean almost anything from "oops" to "let's celebrate!"
- *Shaggin' the drag*—driving up and down Main Street, usually on a Friday night
- *Quad*—the Quad Cities (Davenport and Bettendorf in Iowa, and Moline and Rock Island in Illinois)

HOW TO EAT LIKE AN IOWAN

Immigrants to Iowa brought their favorite recipes with them, and common dishes in Iowa reflect this background. In Cedar Rapids, where Czech and other eastern European people settled, you might get *kolaches* in the bakeries. In Dutch-settled Pella, ask for pastries made with marzipan (almond paste)—they're called Dutch letters. In Elk Horn, the Danish restaurants will serve *rødkal*, which is red cabbage, probably accompanying a pork dish. At Guatemalan restaurants in Decorah, people dine on *cajon*, chicken in a spicy green sauce.

Assorted marzipan treats

MENU

WHAT'S ON THE MENU IN IOWA?

★ ★ ★

Corn on
the cob

Corn on the Cob

Corn is what Iowa is known for, and sweet corn right out of the field is one of the great flavors of late summer and early autumn.

Muscatine Melon

For a few weeks each summer, Muscatine is famous for its own variety of melon. It's a type of extra-sweet cantaloupe that's great fresh off the vine.

Maytag Blue Cheese

Wheels of creamy blue cheese have been produced by the Maytag Dairy Farms in Newton since 1941. The farm ages the cheese, regarded as some of the world's best, for many months in the natural caves nearby.

Mettwurst

Mettwurst is a type of sausage brought to western Iowa by German settlers. Each settlement, even each family, had its own recipe for this sausage. Today, many Iowa families still produce these delicious sausages.

Tamales

Iowans of every ancestry love this Mexican dish. Tamales are cornmeal dough filled with meat or cheese. The dough is wrapped in a corn husk and then steamed.

Tamales

TRY THIS RECIPE
Quick Corn Chowder

On a chilly winter night, this easy-to-make corn chowder will warm you up. Have an adult nearby to help.

Ingredients:

¼ pound bacon, cut in small pieces, about ½ inch wide

1 small onion, peeled and thinly sliced

2 medium potatoes, peeled and cut into cubes about ½ inch square

1 can (12 ounces) evaporated milk

2 cans (14¾ ounces each) creamed corn

Salt and pepper to taste

Instructions:

1. Put the bacon pieces in a frying pan over medium-high heat. Cook, stirring every few minutes, until they are lightly browned. Be careful not to get spattered by grease.
2. Add the onion and continue to cook, stirring occasionally, until the onion is almost transparent.
3. Add the cubed potatoes plus just enough water to cover them. Cover the pan and let the potatoes cook until you can put a fork in them easily.
4. Add the evaporated milk, creamed corn, and salt and pepper to taste.
5. Continue heating the mixture, stirring every few minutes, until it's hot. Serves 4.

GRANT WOOD: IOWA ARTIST

Iowa's farmland, farmers, and high-ways were in Grant Wood's soul, and they appeared regularly in his paintings. Wood (1891–1942) was born in Anamosa, raised in Cedar Rapids, and later taught painting at the University of Iowa. His American Gothic is one of the nation's most recognizable paintings. It shows a scowling Iowa farmer holding a pitchfork standing next to a woman. When the painting was first exhibited, people were not sure whether Wood was being critical or affectionate toward the farmers. People remain unsure today.

? **Want to know more?** Visit www.factsfornow .scholastic.com and enter the keyword **Iowa**.

THE ARTS

Iowa has a strong history of supporting town bands. In 1922, Karl L. King, a band-music composer, persuaded the state to pass a law letting towns charge a small tax to support a town band. King directed the Iowa State Fair Band from 1921 to 1959. Composer Meredith Willson of Mason City com-

Writer Hamlin Garland in his study, 1890

memorated band music and Iowa in the musical *The Music Man*, which features the song "Seventy-Six Trombones." The versatile Willson also wrote the University of Iowa fight song.

Iowa has inspired many artists and writers. Grant Wood painted pictures of farmers and their farmland. Hamlin Garland invented the term "Middle Border" for Iowa's frontier region, where he lived when he was young. In the Middle Border, safety seemed to end at the edge of town. His books about his life and what it was like to live in Iowa in the late 19th century include *A Son of the Middle Border* and the Pulitzer Prize–winning *A Daughter of the Middle Border*.

Few people know the name Mildred Augustine Wirt Benson, but many children have read her books. Benson, a native of Ladora, wrote the first 23 Nancy Drew mysteries using the name Carolyn Keene.

MINI-BIO

ANN LANDERS AND ABIGAIL VAN BUREN: DOUBLE THE ADVICE

Esther Pauline (1918–2002) and Pauline Esther (1918–2013) Friedman were identical twins born in Sioux City. The question of who was who continued throughout their lives. In 1955, Esther (seen here) became an advice columnist writing under the name Ann Landers (she took over an existing column from a woman who had died), and the following year, Pauline became Abigail Van Buren in her new advice column called "Dear Abby." They competed for many years, answering the same kinds of questions in newspapers all over North America. Pauline's daughter, Jeanne Phillips, has been writing the "Dear Abby" column since 2002.

? **Want to know more?** Visit www.factsfornow.scholastic.com and enter the keyword **Iowa**.

Iowans read more books per person than people in any other state.

SPORTS AND CELEBRATIONS

Iowa doesn't have any major sports teams, but fans cheer on its AAA minor league baseball team, the Iowa Cubs, who play in Des Moines. Des Moines is also home to the Iowa Barnstormers, an arena football team.

SEE IT HERE!

BUILD IT AND THEY WILL COME

Just outside of Dyersville is a farm where a cornfield has been turned into a baseball diamond. Author William Patrick Kinsella (a Canadian who studied writing in Iowa) wrote a novel called *Shoeless Joe*, which was made into a movie called *Field of Dreams*. It's the story of an Iowa farmer in financial trouble. After he hears a mysterious voice say, "If you build it, he will come," he plows up his field and builds a major league baseball diamond. He is certain that Shoeless Joe Jackson, a great baseball player from the early part of the 1900s, will come and play. The movie was filmed on this Dyersville farm, and the baseball diamond is still there. Visitors are welcome to play on it.

Some Iowans claim that the first inter-collegiate football game ever played west of the Mississippi took place in 1889 between Grinnell College and the University of Iowa. Today, there are three big Iowa sports college teams: the University of Iowa Hawkeyes, the Iowa State Cyclones, and the University of Northern Iowa Panthers.

Almost every small town in Iowa has a baseball field, where children learn to play and adults engage in friendly games. The movie *Field of Dreams* was filmed at a baseball field built near Dyersville.

Many Iowans also enjoy bicycling. Since 1973, the *Des Moines Register* newspaper has

Visitors play and watch games at the Dyersville baseball diamond where the movie *Field of Dreams* was filmed.

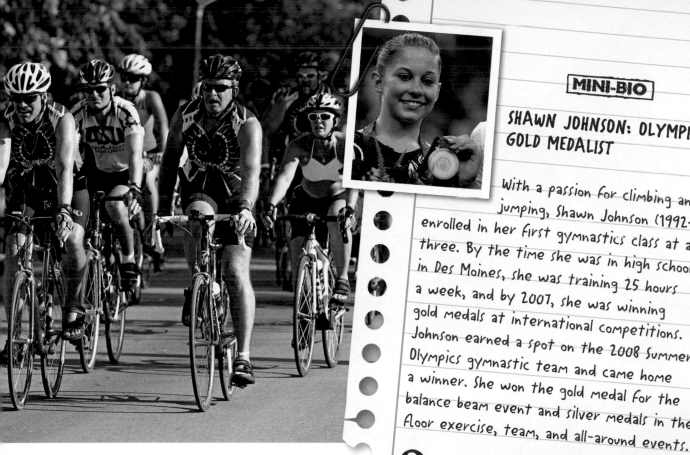

MINI-BIO

SHAWN JOHNSON: OLYMPIC GOLD MEDALIST

With a passion for climbing and jumping, Shawn Johnson (1992–) enrolled in her first gymnastics class at age three. By the time she was in high school in Des Moines, she was training 25 hours a week, and by 2007, she was winning gold medals at international competitions. Johnson earned a spot on the 2008 Summer Olympics gymnastic team and came home a winner. She won the gold medal for the balance beam event and silver medals in the floor exercise, team, and all-around events.

? Want to know more? Visit www.factsfornow .scholastic.com and enter the keyword **Iowa**.

Participants in the Register's Annual Great Bicycle Ride Across Iowa

sponsored a seven-day race in July called the Register's Annual Great Bicycle Ride Across Iowa. So many people want to participate that a lottery is held each year to decide who gets to be among the 8,500 riders.

Davenport holds the Bix 7, a running race held the same weekend as the Bix Beiderbecke Memorial Jazz Festival in July. Each year, between 15,000 and 20,000 people run—or walk—the 7-mile (11 km) course on the steep hills of the river city.

THE GREAT LAWN MOWER RIDE

In the autumn of 1994, 73-year-old Alvin Straight of Laurens set out to visit his ailing brother across the Mississippi in Wisconsin. He couldn't drive a car because his eyesight was bad, and he didn't have the money for an airplane ticket. So instead, he used his lawn mower to travel the 240 miles (386 km) to Mt. Zion, Wisconsin. At 5 miles an hour (8 kph), the journey took six weeks. Alvin died in 1996 before director David Lynch made his story into a film, *The Straight Story*.

READ ABOUT

The Iowa state legislature meets in 2014.

CHAPTER SEVEN

GOVERNMENT

★

"WE HAVE A LONG TRADITION IN THIS STATE OF CARING FOR OUR NEIGHBORS," SAID FORMER GOVERNOR TOM VILSACK. Citizens make their wishes known to the state government, and the government helps Iowans in as many ways as it can. Government workers do this, too. Teachers educate children, and social workers ensure their safety. A special commission encourages Latino Iowans to open businesses. And archaeologists and historians preserve the state's past.

The state capitol in Des Moines

THE CAPITAL AND THE CONSTITUTION

Iowa became its own territory in 1838. For the first three years, the town of Burlington was the capital. Then a new site on the banks of the Iowa River was chosen for the capital. Lawmakers called it Iowa City. But only a few years later, legislators decided they should be closer to the center of the state. In 1857, they moved the capital to the booming city of Des Moines.

FAQ

Q: **WHAT DOES *DES MOINES* MEAN?**

A: The capital city is named after the Des Moines River, but no one is quite sure where the river got its name. It might mean "river of the monks" in French. More likely, French traders used it as a shortened version of Rivière des Moingwena, meaning "river of the Moingwena," after the Native American group. The name could also have come from *de moyen*, meaning "middle," since the river is midway between the Mississippi and Missouri rivers.

The capitol building in Des Moines at the time was rather plain and uninteresting. By 1870, legislators wanted a new building that they believed would better represent their growing state. The construction of today's capitol started in 1871 and took 15 years. Today's capitol has five domes, the largest of which is covered in gold.

The state constitution established three branches of government, like the federal government. Iowa's state government consists of the executive, legislative, and judicial branches.

Capital City

This map shows places of interest in Des Moines, Iowa's capital city.

CAPITOL FACTS

Here are some fascinating facts about Iowa's state capitol.

- Year completed: 1886
- Original cost: $2,873,294.59
- Exterior dimensions: 365 feet (111 m) from north to south; 247 feet (75 m) from east to west
- Number of different types of marble used in the interior: 29
- Number of fireplaces in the building: 24
- Height of central dome: 275 feet (84 m) above the ground floor
- Diameter of dome: 80 feet (24 m)

Iowa State Government

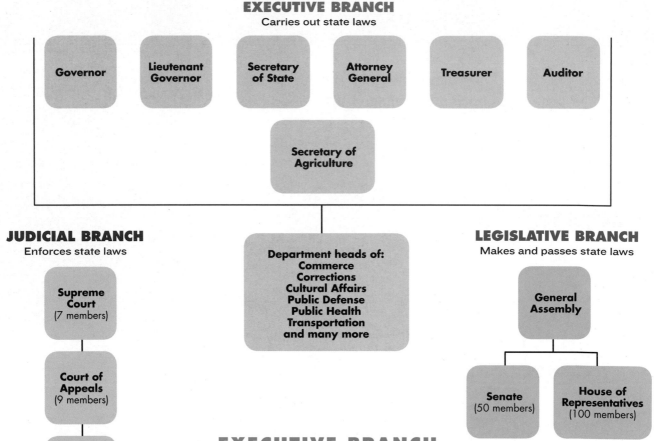

EXECUTIVE BRANCH
Carries out state laws

Governor

Lieutenant Governor

Secretary of State

Attorney General

Treasurer

Auditor

Secretary of Agriculture

JUDICIAL BRANCH
Enforces state laws

Supreme Court
(7 members)

Court of Appeals
(9 members)

District Courts
(8 districts)

Department heads of:
Commerce
Corrections
Cultural Affairs
Public Defense
Public Health
Transportation
and many more

LEGISLATIVE BRANCH
Makes and passes state laws

General Assembly

Senate
(50 members)

House of Representatives
(100 members)

EXECUTIVE BRANCH

The executive branch carries out, or executes, the laws of the state. It is headed by the governor, who is elected to a four-year term. The governor has many duties. He or she appoints the heads of departments and commissions that do the work of the state. The governor also represents Iowa in trying to bring new business to the state.

Other elected state officials include the lieutenant governor, who takes over if the governor can no longer serve; the secretary of state, who oversees elections; the auditor, who keeps track of the state's finances; the treasurer, who invests the state's money; the attorney general, who is in

Governor Terry Branstad signs a bill in 2013.

charge of legal affairs for the state; and the secretary of agriculture. The executive branch also includes more than 20 departments that specialize in areas such as natural resources, agriculture, and transportation.

LEGISLATIVE BRANCH

The legislative branch, called the Iowa General Assembly, makes the laws of the state. It consists of two bodies, the house of representatives and the senate. The 100 representatives serve two-year terms, while the 50 senators serve four-year terms. The legislature meets only from January to late April or early May each year, which gives the representatives and senators time to hold other jobs.

Representing Iowa

This list shows the number of elected officials who represent Iowa, both on the state and national levels.

OFFICE	NUMBER	LENGTH OF TERM
State senators	50	4 years
State representatives	100	2 years
U.S. senators	2	6 years
U.S. representatives	4	2 years
Presidential electors	6	—

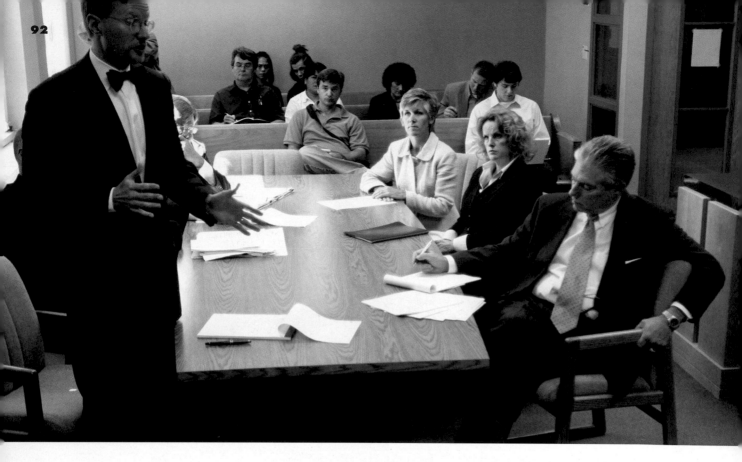

A lawyer addresses the court at a hearing in Waukon.

JUDICIAL BRANCH

The judicial branch is the court system, which makes certain that laws are followed. Most trials in Iowa are held in a district court. If people involved in the case think the district court made a mistake, they can ask the court of appeals to review the decision. The Iowa Supreme Court, the highest court in the state, can review decisions made by the court of appeals.

The governor appoints the seven members of the supreme court and the nine members of the court of appeals for one year. After that, citizens vote on whether to retain the judges in office. Supreme court justices are elected to eight-year terms, while court of appeals judges serve six-year terms. They may continue to be re-elected until they turn 72, when they must retire.

LOCAL GOVERNMENT

Iowa has 99 counties, each run by an elected board of supervisors. County officials collect property taxes, plan county parks, and oversee elections. The county sheriff oversees law enforcement in the areas of a county that are not within towns or cities.

VOTING FIRST

The winter before each presidential election, eyes across the nation turn toward Iowa because Iowa provides the first

A police officer shares information with residents after the 2008 flood in Cedar Rapids.

MINI-BIO

HERBERT HOOVER: IOWA'S PRESIDENT

Herbert Hoover (1874–1964), a native of West Branch, was the nation's 31st president and the first president born west of the Mississippi. He moved to Oregon to live with an uncle after his parents died. Hoover became a successful mining engineer. During and after World War I, he received wide acclaim for his humanitarian work, coordinating efforts that fed millions of starving people in Europe. He became president in 1929, a few months before the Great Depression began. Many people thought he did too little to improve the economy and help suffering Americans, and he lost the 1932 election to Franklin D. Roosevelt.

? Want to know more? Visit www.factsfornow.scholastic.com and enter the keyword **Iowa**.

President Barack Obama visits with voters at the 2012 Iowa State Fair.

WORD TO KNOW

caucuses *closed political meetings, often to choose a candidate*

view of who might become the presidential candidates. For weeks or even months before Iowans vote, candidates travel the state, talking with citizens.

Many states use primary elections to choose their political party nominee for president. Iowa does it differently. Iowa holds **caucuses**, where voters stand up and say their choice. If a candidate gets less than 15 percent of the vote, he or she is eliminated and supporters can change their votes to more successful candidates. Journalist Kent Garber says, "The act of caucusing is part dodge ball (don't get eliminated), part tug of war (bring opponents to your side), and part high school popularity contest (have the most followers)."

Why does Iowa get to be the first chooser in a presidential election? In 2008, political writer Steven Thomma wrote in the McClatchy newspapers, "Why not Iowa? For one thing, it's small enough that candidates can meet

Iowa Counties

This map shows the 99 counties in Iowa. Des Moines, the state capital, is indicated with a star.

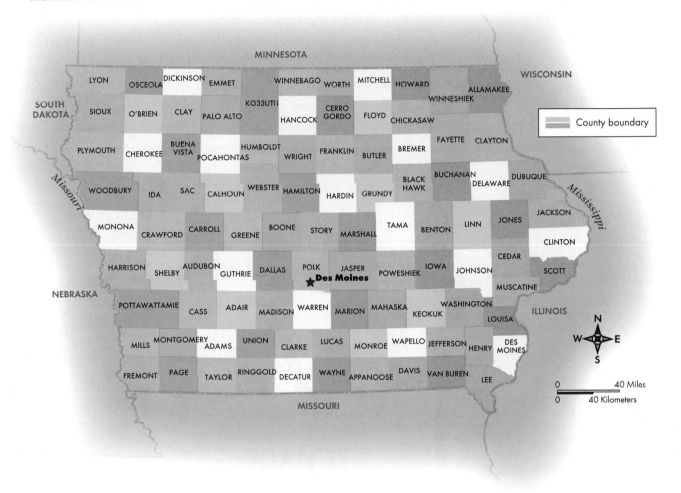

people face to face in living rooms and coffee shops. Those people ask questions about what's on their minds, not necessarily what the news media think is important or what the campaigns have polled and researched." At the 2008 Iowa caucuses, Democrats chose Barack Obama, marking the first time Iowans had favored an African American presidential candidate. He went on to become the first African American president of the United States.

State Flag

Iowa had been a state for nearly 75 years when the legislature adopted the state flag in 1921. Knoxville resident Dixie Cornell Gebhardt designed the flag. It features three vertical stripes of blue, white, and red. The blue symbolizes loyalty, justice, and truth; the white symbolizes purity; and the red symbolizes courage. On the white stripe is an eagle carrying blue streamers inscribed with the state motto, "Our liberties we prize and our rights we will maintain." The word *Iowa* is in red letters just below the streamers.

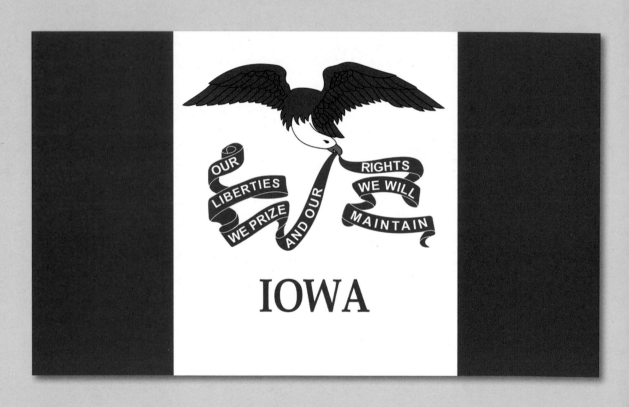

State Seal

One of the initial acts of the first Iowa legislature in 1847 was to adopt the Great Seal of Iowa. The seal features a citizen soldier standing in a wheat field, surrounded by farming and industrial tools. The Mississippi River is in the background. An eagle is overhead, holding in its beak a scroll bearing the state motto.

READ ABOUT

An Iowa farmer discusses his plants with two crop consultants.

CHAPTER EIGHT

ECONOMY

★

IOWA IS HOME TO THE MOST PRODUCTIVE FARMS IN THE WORLD. But agriculture requires fewer workers than it did in the past. Today, less than 5 percent of people who work in Iowa are involved in farming. Many more people work in manufacturing, transportation, education, and the arts.

A field of corn being fertilized

Iowa produces more corn and soybeans than any other state.

Q8 WHAT'S A "BUTTER COW LADY?"

A8 She is the person who sculpts a life-sized cow out of butter for the Iowa State Fair. The longest-serving butter cow lady was Duffy Lyon of Toledo, who did the job from 1960 to 2006.

SERVICE INDUSTRIES

People who work in service industries do things for other people. Service industries include everything from banking to child care. Your teacher works in the service industry. So does the bus driver who takes you to school, the clerk at the ice cream parlor, and the doctor who sets your broken arm. Today, services employ far more people than manufacturing or agriculture.

FROM THE FARM

Farmland covers just over 90 percent of Iowa. Iowa has the third-highest total value of farm output among the states. It is part of America's breadbasket, a group of states with rich soil that produces much of the nation's crops. Iowa's most valuable product is corn. Farmers often alternate planting corn and soybeans, which puts valuable nutrients back in the soil. Iowa farmers also grow hay, oats, wheat, and apples. Most of the state's dairy farms are in the northeast.

WOW

Jesse Hiatt of Madison County developed the Red Delicious apple in the 1870s. It's the best-selling apple in North America.

JESSIE FIELD SHAMBAUGH: INSPIRATIONAL TEACHER

Jessie Field Shambaugh (1881–1971) developed her students' love of learning by offering them fascinating hands-on projects that related to their farm environment. At her school in Page County, she set up boys and girls clubs teaching agriculture, gardening, cooking, and sewing. Soon, her after-school programs spread throughout the state, becoming the 4-H movement. Today, 4-H is a youth organization administered by the U.S. government, which teaches farming, science, engineering, and technology. It has 6.5 million members.

? **Want to know more?** Visit www.factsfornow .scholastic.com and enter the keyword **Iowa**.

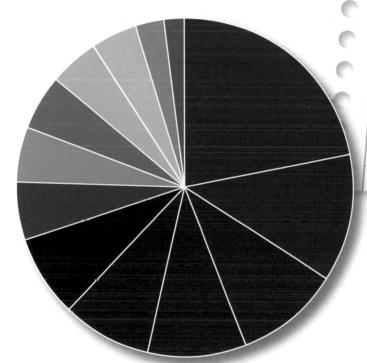

What Do Iowans Do?

This color-coded chart shows what industries Iowans work in.

- **23.9%** Educational services, and health care and social assistance 372,756
- **14.7%** Manufacturing 229,557
- **11.7%** Retail trade 181,666
- **7.7%** Finance and insurance, and real estate and rental and leasing 119,357
- **7.6%** Arts, entertainment, and recreation, and accommodation and food services 118,557
- **6.8%** Professional, scientific, and management, and administrative and waste management services 106,174
- **6.1%** Construction 95,581
- **4.7%** Transportation and warehousing, and utilities 73,661
- **4.4%** Other services, except public administration 68,747
- **4.0%** Agriculture, forestry, fishing and hunting, and mining 62,188
- **3.3%** Public administration 51,853
- **3.0%** Wholesale trade 46,372
- **2.0%** Information 30,862

Source: U.S. Census Bureau, 2010 census

Major Agricultural and Mining Products

This map shows where Iowa's major agricultural and mining products come from. See a cow? That means cattle are raised there.

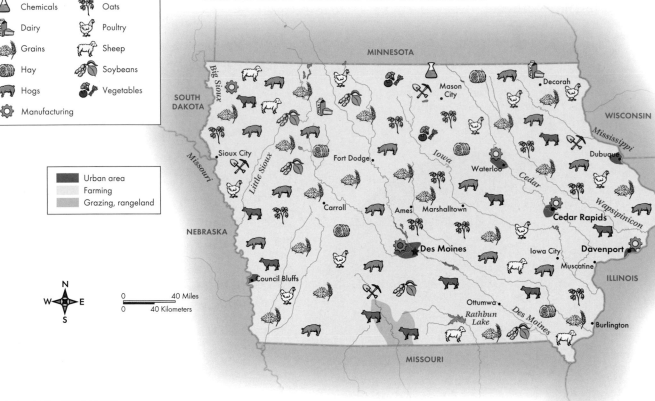

Cattle
Chemicals
Dairy
Grains
Hay
Hogs
Manufacturing
Mineral mining
Oats
Poultry
Sheep
Soybeans
Vegetables

Urban area
Farming
Grazing, rangeland

WORD TO KNOW

ethanol *an alcohol used as a gasoline substitute, made by fermenting corn or other material*

Top Products

Agriculture Corn, hogs, soybeans, beef cattle, milk, chickens, hay, oats, wheat, apples

Manufacturing Food processing, computers, farm machinery, motor homes, chemicals, aerospace equipment

Mining Limestone, clay, gypsum, sand and gravel

MADE IN IOWA

Food processing is a major industry in Iowa. Grains are made into breakfast cereal in Cedar Rapids, and Sioux City is a center of meatpacking. More than half of the corn grown in Iowa is turned into **ethanol**, a gasoline substitute. In 2013, Iowa had 42 plants making ethanol, more than any other state. Together, they account for nearly 30 percent of all ethanol production in the United States. Iowans also make aerospace equipment, chemicals, motor vehicles, and computers.

Arthur A. Collins founded the Collins Radio Company in Cedar Rapids in 1933. Today, the company is known as Rockwell Collins and provides the radio communication for many airplanes and the U.S. space program. Ted Waitt started the Gateway Corporation in 1985 on his family's farm near Sioux City in western Iowa. It was a cattle ranch,

In 2007, Dario Franchitti won the Indianapolis 500 driving a car powered completely by ethanol.

Filling Up Your Car on Iowa Fuel

These days, a big word in farming communities is *ethanol*. Many people hope that ethanol, a gasoline substitute most often made from corn, will decrease the amount of oil the United States has to buy from foreign countries. Ethanol is rarely used alone, but many people promote the use of E85, which is a combination of 85 percent ethanol to 15 percent gasoline for use in automobiles.

Pros

The use of a crop for making ethanol will give farmers in poor areas of the country a market for their corn. It could help relieve the U.S. dependence on oil from foreign countries. Brazil has stopped importing almost all oil by making ethanol from sugarcane; perhaps the United States can do the same with corn. And the fuel is renewable. Senator Richard Lugar of Indiana has said, "Ethanol is a premier, high performance fuel. It has tremendous environmental benefits and is a key component to energy independence for our country."

Cons

It takes a lot of chemicals to grow corn, harming the soil and the air. The process of making ethanol requires burning fuel, usually coal, which puts more pollutants into the atmosphere. It also takes a great deal of water. Dan Becker of the Sierra Club explains the problems: "It's very energy-intensive to create ethanol. A lot of diesel fuel is used to cultivate the corn; a lot of . . . fossil fuels are used to distill it into ethanol." Also farmers are planting so much corn for ethanol that not as many food crops are being planted. This has raised the price of food.

Workers on an assembly line at a Winnebago factory in Forest City

THE FIRST ELECTRIC CAR

William Morrison of Des Moines built what was probably the first electric car in the world in 1887. He converted a buggy to run on electricity from the batteries he was producing. It could reach 14 mph (23 kph), even though each of the 24 batteries weighed 32 pounds (15 kilograms). A Chicagoan who bought the rights to the "automobile" raced it in the nation's first automobile race, held in 1896, and won!

so for years he used the black-and-white design of a cow on the box bearing the computers that he shipped to customers. Winnebago motor homes have been made in Winnebago County since the mid-1950s. A local businessman and other community people persuaded a small California company to make travel trailers there. By 1986, Winnebago Industries was a Fortune 500 company, meaning it is one of the biggest businesses in the country. Today, Winnebago also makes farm trailers and buses.

In 1893, F. L. Maytag of Newton put together several small investors to form a company that made farm equipment. In 1907, they started making washing machines so they would have a product that sold when farm equipment didn't. For decades, Maytag appliances were made in Newton. Then in 2006, the Whirlpool Corporation bought Maytag and shipped the work to Benton Harbor, Michigan. Although Newton lost its Maytag factory, a new factory there employs 500 people to manufacture wind turbine blades.

Some of the blades made in Newton are used in Iowa, as are blades manufactured by Siemens in Fort Madison. Other companies in Iowa make turbines, towers, and other parts for wind turbines. MidAmerican Energy has been building wind farms in northern Iowa since 2004 and is aiming to supply electricity made by wind power to almost 400,000 homes. Only Texas and California have more wind farms than Iowa. Wind farms are most commonly found in the northern and western parts of the state.

MINING

Coal was found in Iowa along the Des Moines River in the 1840s, but it wasn't mined in great quantities until the railroads started coming through. They needed to burn coal to make steam to power their engines. In all, coal was mined in 34 southern Iowa counties. Those mines have all been abandoned, and no coal is mined in Iowa today. Lead mining is also a thing of the past because the mines had to be so deep to reach the remaining ore that they filled with water.

The major mineral mined today is limestone for use in construction. Stone City got its name from the huge limestone deposits located there. Gypsum is a mineral used primarily in making cement and in drywall, which is also used in construction. Iowa's main deposits of the mineral are located near Fort Dodge.

MINI-BIO

JOHN L. LEWIS: LABOR LEADER

John L. Lewis (1880–1969) was born in a coal-mining camp near Lucas. His experiences in the Iowa and Illinois coal mines, starting when he was a teenager, led him to become one of the major labor organizers in American history. As acting president of the United Mine Workers in 1919, he called for the first major strike against coal mines. Four hundred thousand workers walked off their jobs. That time, they didn't gain anything by their strike, but later Lewis was able to improve both wages and safety for mine workers.

? Want to know more? Visit www.factsfornow.scholastic.com and enter the keyword **Iowa**.

WORD TO KNOW

strike *an organized refusal to work, usually as a sign of protest about working conditions*

Interstate highway 35

N W E S

MINNESOTA
SOUTH DAKOTA
WISCONSIN
NEBRASKA
ILLINOIS
MISSOURI

Big Sioux
Missouri
Little Sioux
Iowa
Cedar
Mississippi
Wapsipinicon
Des Moines
Rathbun Lake

Sioux Center
Estherville
Spencer
Orange City
Clear Lake
Mason City
Burr Oak
Decorah
Spillville
Festina
Le Mars
Cherokee
Algona
Charles City
Nashua
Strawberry Point
Storm Lake
Webster City
Waverly
Cedar Falls
Manchester
Dubuque
Sioux City
Fort Dodge
Waterloo
Independence
Dyersville
Geographic Center of Iowa
Gladbrook
Vinton
Anamosa
Sabula
Denison
Carroll
Boone
Marshalltown
Tama
Amana Colonies
Marion
Cedar Rapids
Clinton
Perry
Ames
West Branch
Ankeny
Grinnell
Coralville
Davenport
Le Claire
Harlan
Elk Horn
Johnston
Iowa City
Riverside
74
Van Meter
Des Moines
Pella
Kalona
280
Muscatine
Greenfield
Winterset
235
Washington
Indianola
Oskaloosa
Wapello
Council Bluffs
Glenwood
Creston
Ottumwa
Fairfield
Mt. Pleasant
Red Oak
35
Burlington
29
Shenandoah
Clarinda
Centerville
Fort Madison
Keokuk

29
680
80

0   40 Miles
0   40 Kilometers

CHAPTER NINE

TRAVEL GUIDE

★

IOWA SEEMS TO HAVE SOMETHING FOR EVERYONE. There are museums about everything from motorcycles to airplanes to pearl buttons. You can take a boat ride on the Mississippi, dance at a powwow, and search for fossils. There's a lot to do and see, so grab your map and follow along as we travel through the Hawkeye State.

←—Follow along with this travel map. We'll start in Des Moines, circle the state, and end in Council Bluffs.

DES MOINES AREA

THINGS TO DO: Discover what life was like on a pioneer farm, take a ride on an old-time train, and get a good look at butterflies.

★ **Iowa State Capitol:** The capitol is an elaborate building with five domes. Displays include 138 Civil War flags carried into battle and dolls wearing tiny replicas of the gowns of Iowa's first ladies.

★ **State Historical Society:** See exhibits about the people, places, and events that have impacted Iowa history.

★ **Living History Farms:** At this site, you can explore an Ioway farm from 1700 and a pioneer farm from 1850. An 1875 farming town, Walnut Hill, has also been re-created.

Living History Farms

★ **Science Center of Iowa:** Explore the world of science, from space to dinosaurs, with hands-on exhibits, live programs and demonstrations, and a state-of-the art planetarium. Don't forget to see a show at the center's six-story IMAX theater!

Boone

★ **Boone & Scenic Valley Railroad:** Steam through the Des Moines River valley on an old-time train.

Ames

★ **Reiman Gardens:** Walk among rare and beautiful butterflies in the Christina Reiman Butterfly Wing building, which is shaped like a butterfly in flight. It contains living butterflies from six continents.

FAQ

Q: IS THERE A CAROUSEL IN IOWA?

A: Story City is the only town in Iowa that owns a carousel. Its original owners brought it to Story City each year starting in 1913 for the Fourth of July celebration. The town bought the carousel in 1938.

Pella Historical Village

Pella

★ **Pella Historical Village:** At this village that re-creates Holland of long ago, you can see windmills and 21 Dutch-style buildings. You can even try on traditional Dutch wooden shoes.

Van Meter

★ **Bob Feller Museum:** Look for an old red barn on the farm where Bob Feller, whom some people call the greatest pitcher ever, learned to play baseball. As a 17-year-old rookie for the Cleveland Indians, Feller struck out eight players in three innings.

Indianola

★ **National Balloon Museum:** This is where Iowa's first U.S. National Ballooning championship was held in 1970. Giant hot air balloons fill the sky during the nine days of the National Balloon Classic each summer.

Winterset

★ **Covered bridges:** At one time, Madison County had 19 covered bridges, but today only six remain. Each October, Winterset hosts the Covered Bridge Festival.

★ **John Wayne Birthplace:** John Wayne starred in many classic Western movies. The small home where he was born in 1907 has been restored to what it would have looked like in that year.

SOUTHEAST

THINGS TO DO: Walk the nation's "crookedest street," explore an island in the Mississippi, and learn about Buffalo Bill.

Davenport

★ **Figge Art Museum:** At this museum, you can laugh along with Grant Wood's sister Nan, who posed as the woman in *American Gothic*. She collected parodies of the painting, which are now on display here.

Burlington

★ **Snake Alley:** Snake Alley was built in 1894 to connect Burlington's downtown with a business district on top of the bluff. The hope was that horses would be able to climb

Snake Alley

the street. The brick-paved twisty road proved unsuccessful with the horses, but today it draws many visitors. It is often called the "crookedest street in the world," though many people argue that a street in San Francisco is more crooked.

FAQ

Q: HOW MANY CITIES ARE IN THE QUAD CITIES?

A: If you guessed four, you might be wrong, even though *quad* means "four." Many people think there are actually five small cities near each other. Two are in Iowa—Davenport and Bettendorf—and the others are in Illinois: Rock Island, Moline, and East Moline. (It's East Moline that gets left out.) Davenport is the largest of the Quad Cities.

Muscatine

★ **Pearl Button Museum:** You can see how buttons were once made from clamshells collected on the bottom of the Mississippi River. In the 1890s, Muscatine became the largest manufacturer of pearl buttons in the world.

In 1898, Iowa produced 138,615,696 buttons!

BUTTON MAKER

John Boepple, a farmworker near Muscatine, had been a button maker in Europe. One day, he discovered clam and mussel shells in the Mississippi River. Impressed by their look of pearl, he made some buttons out of the shells. In 1895, he started making pearl buttons, and Muscatine soon became the button capital of the world, producing more buttons than any other city.

Boepple Button Company, late 1800s

Coralville

★ **Devonian Fossil Gorge:** The Great Flood of 1993 swept clean the spillway of Coralville Dam, revealing limestone rock from 375 million years ago. Fossils embedded in the rock stand out. Since then, it's been kept clear for geology enthusiasts.

Sabula

★ **Island City:** The town takes up most of the island of Sabula in the Mississippi River. Fewer than a thousand people live on the island, where you can take a swim in the Mississippi River and explore the Green Island State Wildlife Refuge.

West Branch

★ **Herbert Hoover National Historic Site:** Here you can visit the tiny two-room house where the 31st president was born in 1874. The presidential library holds photos and artifacts of his life.

Herbert Hoover National Historic Site

Riverside

★ **Star Trek:** According to the TV series *Star Trek*, Captain James T. Kirk was born in Riverside, near Kalona, on March 22, 2233. The town holds a huge Trek Fest each year, and a replica of the Starship *Enterprise* is located in the town park.

Amana Colonies

★ **German Villages:** There are seven Amana villages, and each has a different flavor. Don't miss the video at the historical museum in Main Amana to find out more about the people who settled these villages.

Kalona

★ **Kalona Historical Village and Mennonite Museum:** This village is filled with restored buildings from 19th-century Iowa. You can watch cheese being made, and maybe sample some, and see examples of extraordinary quilts.

Mt. Pleasant

★ **Midwest Old Threshers Heritage Museums:** A collection of small museums celebrate rural Midwestern history. Displays cover agricultural machinery, dolls, and family life.

Fort Madison

★ **Old Fort Madison:** In 1808, Fort Madison, the first fort on the Upper Mississippi, opened. After a fire destroyed the fort in 1813, the foundations of the buildings were not seen again until 1965, when they were discovered under a parking lot. Now the fort has been rebuilt, and costumed guides explain what life was like for soldiers and their families.

Wapello

★ **Toolesboro Mounds:** These seven burial mounds overlooking the Iowa River date back about 2,000 years.

Le Claire

★ **Buffalo Bill Museum:** Visit the homestead where Western showman Buffalo Bill Cody was born.

Ottumwa

★ **Airpower Museum:** At this museum, you can get a good look at many antique aircraft and even touch some.

NORTHEAST

THINGS TO DO: Visit a tiny church, see marionettes from *The Sound of Music*, and experience the Underground Railroad.

Dubuque

★ **National Mississippi River Museum and Aquarium:** Check out six large aquariums and exhibits featuring the wildlife and history of the Mississippi River. Visit the boatyard and walk the decks of the *William M. Black* steamboat.

★ **Fenelon Place Elevator:** This has been called the world's shortest and steepest railroad, rising 189 feet (58 m) over the course of a 296-foot-long (90 m) track. It was built in 1882 so that a wealthy banker could quickly get home for lunch and then back to work. It has burned and been replaced twice.

Fenelon Place Elevator

Dyersville

★ **National Farm Toy Museum:**
Imagine 30,000 tractors and trucks
and other farm machines all in one
place. These are miniature replicas,
and they're here because three of the
world's major farm toy makers are
located around Dyersville.

Anamosa

★ **National Motorcycle Museum:** See
more than 225 motorcycles built from
1903 to 1975.

Cedar Rapids

★ **National Czech and Slovak
Museum and Library:** Learn about
the heritage of the Czech and Slovak
people who settled the region, and
admire artifacts such as *kroje*, traditional costumes worn by some who
immigrated to Iowa.

★ **African American Museum of
Iowa:** Learn the story of African
Americans in Iowa and discover the
brave people who were part of the
Underground Railroad.

Tama

★ **Meskwaki Museum:** Opened in
2011, this museum tells the story of
the Meskwaki people through photographs, maps, and artifacts, including drums, clothing, headdresses,
and other historical items.

A model of Harry Potter's Hogwarts School of Witchcraft
and Wizardry, made from 602,200 matchsticks

Gladbrook

★ **Matchstick Marvels:** Patience
and nimble fingers are required to
build big objects out of tiny wooden
matchsticks. Since 1977, Iowa artist
Patrick Acton has used more than
4 million matchsticks—and lots of
glue—to build his marvels.

Waterloo

★ **National Wrestling Hall of Fame
Dan Gable Museum:** Legends of
wrestling are highlighted in the Hall
of Fame.

Mason City

★ **Charles H. MacNider Art
Museum:** Are you a fan of the film
The Sound of Music? You can see
the marionettes used in the von
Trapp children's marionette show
here. They were created by puppet
makers Bil and Cora Baird.

Nashua

★ **Old Bradford Pioneer Village Museum:** Settled in 1840, Bradford was originally an Indian trading post. Today, some original cabins and furnishings have been preserved.

Spillville

★ **Bily Clocks Museum:** Here you can see many large, magnificent wooden clocks carved by Iowa's Bily brothers.

Burr Oak

★ **Laura Ingalls Wilder Museum:** Visit the house where children's book author Laura Ingalls Wilder lived in 1876, after a grasshopper plague drove her family out of Minnesota.

Festina

★ **World's Tiniest Church:** More officially known as St. Anthony of Padua Chapel, this church was built in 1885 by the mother of a soldier who promised God that she would build a chapel if her son survived the war he was fighting. It measures just 14 by 20 feet (4.3 by 6 m) and seats eight people, two each in four pews.

Decorah

★ **Vesterheim Norwegian-American Museum:** This museum features 16 historic buildings that recall the life of the region's early Norwegian settlers.

Strawberry Point

★ **Wilder Memorial Museum:** This museum is filled with treasures, including 800 antique dolls, lamps, farm tools, and much more.

NORTHWEST

THINGS TO DO: Scream for ice cream and learn about pioneer days.

Le Mars

★ **Wells' Dairy:** Wells' Dairy, maker of Blue Bunny ice cream, claims to make more ice cream each day than any other place in the world. At the visitors' center, you can learn all about ice cream and enjoy a cone at an old-fashioned ice cream parlor.

Wells' Dairy

Algona

★ **Camp Algona POW Museum:**
Learn what life was like for the German, Italian, and Japanese prisoners of war who were captured overseas during World War II and brought to distant Iowa.

Sioux City

★ **Sioux City Public Museum:**
Explore a log cabin in the style of the pioneer days at this museum dedicated to sharing the region's history. Other exhibits feature Native American clothing and tools as well as the area's wildlife.

SOUTHWEST

THINGS TO DO: Marvel at migrating birds, learn about vintage aircraft, and see a Danish windmill.

Elk Horn

★ **Museum of Danish America:** This museum includes a Danish windmill, which was built in Denmark in 1848, dismantled, and reassembled in Iowa. It also tells about the Danish people who left their homes and started new lives in Iowa. There are special exhibits on Danish arts and culture.

DeSoto National Wildlife Refuge

Missouri Valley

★ **DeSoto National Wildlife Refuge:**
This refuge, which spreads into Nebraska, protects forests, grasslands, wetlands, and other habitat for migrating birds. At the visitors center, you can see cargo that was recovered in 1969 from the steamboat *Bertrand*, which sank in the Missouri River more than 100 years ago.

Greenfield

★ **Iowa Aviation Museum:** This museum displays vintage aircraft and houses the Iowa Aviation Hall of Fame, which profiles Iowans who made a mark in aviation.

Council Bluffs

★ **Western Historic Trails Center:**
Learn about four national historic trails through exhibitions, sculpture, photographs, and a film.

WRITING PROJECTS

TIM

What happened w
This timeline highlig
important events in
state's history—anc
what was happenir
throughout the Unit
at the same time.

GLO

Remember the Wor
Know from the cha
in this book? They'
collected here.

SPORTS TEAMS

★ ★ ★

NCAA Teams (Division I)

Drake University *Bulldogs*
Iowa State University *Cyclones*
University of Iowa *Hawkeyes*
University of Northern Iowa *Panthers*

The University of Iowa football team celebrates a
2008 victory over Iowa State.

CULTURAL INSTITUTIONS

Libraries

The *University of Iowa Libraries* on the university's campus in Iowa City include specialized libraries ranging from art to business. The main library has numerous collections, including the Iowa Women's Archives and the East Asian Collection.

The *Herbert Hoover Presidential Library and Museum* (West Branch) contains not only materials relating to the president but also information on historical eras such as the Roaring Twenties and the Civil War.

The *State Historical Society of Iowa Library*, with collections in Des Moines and Iowa City, offers information on the history of the state and Iowan culture.

Museums

The *Cedar Rapids Museum of Art* holds the world's largest collection of paintings by Grant Wood. Its permanent collection includes more than 5,000 pieces of art.

The *Putnam Museum* (Davenport) features outstanding exhibits on the Mississippi River, Egyptian art, mammals, and much more.

The *Science Center of Iowa* (Des Moines) includes a planetarium and many interactive exhibits on topics ranging from the solar system to the human body.

The *State Historical Museum of Iowa* (Des Moines) houses several exhibits, including one on the end of the ice age complete with a mammoth skeleton.

Performing Arts

The *Des Moines Metro Opera*, founded in 1973, stages more than 100 performances of classical, new, or rarely performed operas each year.

The *Quad City Symphony Orchestra* (Davenport), established in 1916, is the oldest symphony orchestra in Iowa. Each year the orchestra performs six major works, three pops concerts, and three chamber music concerts.

Universities and Colleges

In 2011, Iowa had 3 public and 45 private institutions of higher learning.

ANNUAL EVENTS

January–March

Ice Fest in Dubuque (January)

Okoboji Winter Games (late January)

St. Patrick's Day Celebration in Emmetsburg (second or third weekend in March)

April–June

Drake University Relays in Des Moines (April)

Tulip Festival in Orange City (May)

Tulip Time in Pella (May)

Dubuquefest in Dubuque (mid-May)

Art in the Park in Clinton (June)

Snake Alley Art Fair in Burlington/West Burlington (June)

Grant Wood Art Festival in Stone City (second Sunday in June)

July–September

Riverboat Days in Clinton (early July)

Nordic Fest in Decorah (late July)

The Register's Annual Great Bicycle Ride Across Iowa (late July)

Bix Beiderbecke Memorial Jazz Festival in Davenport (late July/early August)

Iowa Championship Rodeo in Sidney (late July/early August)

National Hobo Convention in Britt (early August)

National Balloon Classic in Indianola (early August)

Meskwaki Indian Powwow in Tama (August)

Iowa State Fair in Des Moines (mid-August)

National Old-Time Country and Bluegrass Festival in Avoca (August)

National Sprint Car Race Championship in Knoxville (mid-August)

Tri-State Rodeo in Fort Madison (early September)

Doll, Toy, Bear Show/Sale in Maquoketa (September)

Guttenberg German Fest (September)

Fort Atkinson Rendezvous (late September)

October–December

Covered Bridge Festival in Madison County (second weekend in October)

Forest Craft Festival in Van Buren County (mid-October)

Livestock shows at the National Cattle Congress in Waterloo (October)

Victorian Christmas in Albia (December)

Ako Abdul-Samad

Ako Abdul-Samad (1948 or 1949–) is the CEO of Creative Visions Human Development Institute in Des Moines. He was elected to the state house of representatives in 2006.

Bess Aldrich (1881–1954), a native of Cedar Falls, took up writing to support her family. She became one of the highest-paid female authors of her time, writing about 200 short stories and 13 novels. She often wrote about Midwestern pioneer women.

Marc Andreessen (1971–) was the technological genius behind Netscape, the first popular Internet browser. He was born in Cedar Falls.

Cap Anson (1852–1922), a native of Marshalltown, is sometimes considered the greatest baseball player of the 19th century. He played for and managed the Chicago White Stockings for 20 years. After he retired, the team became the Chicago Cubs.

Mildred Benson (1905–2002), a native of Ladora, wrote 23 Nancy Drew mysteries between 1930 and 1953 under the name Carolyn Keene. She also wrote children's books under both her own name and other pen names, including Frank Bell, Julia K. Duncan, Helen Louise Thorndyke, and Dorothy West.

Black Hawk See page 41.

Amelia Bloomer (1818–1894) was the first woman to own, operate, and edit a newspaper for women. She lived in Council Bluffs after 1852, leading the fight for women's voting rights in Iowa. Women's loose-fitting pants that she made popular were called bloomers.

Norman Borlaug See page 68.

Bill Bryson (1951–), who was born in Des Moines, has written many travel books. He also wrote a memoir of his Iowa childhood called *The Life and Times of the Thunderbolt Kid*.

Marc Andreessen

RESOURCES

★ ★ ★

BOOKS

Nonfiction

Goodman, Michael E. *Buffalo Bill Cody: Legends of the West*. Mankato, Minn.: Creative Education, 2005.

Jack, Zachary Michael, ed. *Letters to a Young Iowan: Good Sense from the Good Folks of Iowa for Young People Everywhere*. North Liberty, Iowa: Ice Cube Press, 2007.

McCarthy, Ann E. *Critters of Iowa Pocket Guide*. Cambridge, Minn.: Adventure Publications, 2003.

McNeese, Tim. *The Mississippi River*. Philadelphia: Chelsea House, 2004.

Rylant, Cynthia. *Old Town in the Green Groves: Laura Ingalls Wilder's Lost Little House Years*. New York: HarperTrophy, 2007.

Yannuzzi, Della. *Aldo Leopold: Protector of the Wild*. Brookfield, Conn.: Millbrook Press, 2002.

Fiction

Bauer, Joan. *Squashed*. New York: Speak Press, 2005.

Johnston, Tim. *Never So Green*. New York: Farrar, Straus, and Giroux, 2002.

Sheth, Kashmira. *Blue Jasmine*. New York: Hyperion Books for Children, 2004.

Warner, Gertrude Chandler. *The Clue in the Corn Maze*. Morton Grove, Ill.: Albert Whitman, 2004.

FACTS FOR NOW

Visit this Scholastic Web site for more information on Iowa:
www.factsfornow.scholastic.com
Enter the keyword **Iowa**

INDEX

★ ★ ★

AUTHOR'S TIPS AND SOURCE NOTES

★   ★   ★

To research this book, I started at the library. Among the books I counted on were two collections of essays edited by Robert F. Sayre. They were *Take This Exit: Rediscovering the Iowa Landscape* and *Take the Next Exit: New Views of the Iowa Landscape*. Although it's quite old now, *Iowa: A Guide to the Hawkeye State* is always fascinating. It's one of a series of books produced during the Great Depression, when the federal government hired out-of-work writers to create historical and travel guides to each state.